Jewish
Matters

Jewish Matters

A POCKETBOOK OF KNOWLEDGE AND INSPIRATION

Compiled by Doron Kornbluth

TARGUM/FELDHEIM
in conjunction with Jewish Direct

First published 1999
ISBN 1-56871-188-3
Copyright © 1999 by Doron Kornbluth

Phototypeset at Targum Press

Published by:
Targum Press Inc.
22700 W. Eleven Mile Rd.
Southfield, Mich. 48034
email: targum@elronet.co.il
fax: (810)314-7550/toll-free: (888)298-9992

Distributed by:
Feldheim Publishers
200 Airport Executive Park
Nanuet, N.Y. 10954

Printed in Israel

CONTENTS

OUR GOD

לא קם בישראל כמשה עוד
(תפילת ״יגדל״)
Dedicated in loving memory of our grandfather

Rabbi Murry S. Penkower

הרב משה זלמן בן מרדכי מנחם ושרה ז״ל
כ״ג מנחם אב תשנ״ח

A role model for our family and the Jewish people

David and Talya Penkower Roth

Acknowledgments

The idea for this book came from my good friend Andrew Shaw and his team, who, as part of the Education Department of the Union of Jewish Students in Great Britain, published a collection of essays on Jewish themes called *50 Days for 50 Years*. It has deservedly enjoyed great success in Britain. *Jewish Matters*, while very different from its older European sibling, owes itself to *50 Days* in inspiration. Andrew's encouragement of this project was also most helpful.

On behalf of the partners of Jewish Direct, it is my great honor to bring to you the educators and authors who appear in this volume. Many of the them I have been privileged to have as teachers and friends. Others I had no personal connection with until this project. All of them gave of their time and talent to what we all perceive as an important cause: giving all Jews, irrespective of their backgrounds, the opportunity to learn about and fall in love with their heritage.

Throughout my adult life I have been privileged to learn from and be influenced by many exceptional teachers and role models. They are too many and too modest to be acknowledged here but whatever I do of value is attributed to them.

It is appropriate, though, to single out for special thanks those who have been especially helpful in this project: Rabbi Yirmiyohu Abramov, Rabbi Naftoli Kaplan, Rabbi Yosef Kamenetsky, Rabbi Yitzchak Shurin, Rabbi Chaim

Walkin, and Rabbi Joel Zeff. Their guidance kept this book, and me, on track. Special thanks also to Jonathan Bressel of www.ShabbatHospitality.org. In the midst of completing a soon-to-be published guide to the Shabbat table, he has been a constant source of advice and information.

Rabbi Moshe Dombey, Miriam Zakon, D. Liff, Suri Brand, and the rest of the Targum staff have been extremely positive and encouraging. High professional standards matched with a friendly personal touch make Targum a jewel to work with.

Many other people have been of immense help along the way, editing, critiquing, encouraging, vetoing, supporting, and thinking a few steps ahead of me. David and Talya Roth and their families, Tuvia Hoffman, and Barb Horwitz deserve special mention for their contributions. Dozens of other friends and relatives were generous with their time in critiquing essays and suggesting improvements.

My parents and in-laws have been immensely helpful in this project, as they always are. Their everyday concern, support, and love does not go unnoticed, and their specific advice in editing and design was crucial to the completion of *Jewish Matters*. I hope they have much *nachas* from it.

Finally, to my incredible, wonderful wife, Sarah Tikvah: words cannot describe how much I owe her. This is as much her book as mine.

D.K.

P.S. For comments, questions, or to be in touch with the authors, please contact us at: Jewish Matters, P.O. Box 43057, Jerusalem, Israel, or by e-mail at tikvaket@netvision.net.il. Also, check out our Web site: www.jewishmatters.com.

Introduction

I grew up in the beautiful city of Montreal, Canada. Both my parents were born there, and my first ancestors arrived there in 1864 from Europe. Montreal is the metropolis of the province of Quebec, which is 85 percent French-speaking. Yet only a generation ago almost the entire Jewish population of Montreal — over a hundred thousand people — consisted of English-speaking Ashkenazim (Jews of European descent). Today, whenever I visit my parents, I am amazed by the change: now a large minority — I'm told over thirty-thousand — of the Jewish population is made up of French-speaking Jews, mostly from Morocco, who either came directly from there or spent time in France or Israel. And look what they've done! There are many new, beautiful synagogues that have been built and are bursting at the seams. Delicious kosher restaurants abound, mikvehs and Jewish schools, adult classes, study days, trips to Israel. While much of the young Ashkenazic English-speaking population has left, a vibrant Sephardic (Jews from North Africa and the Middle East) Jewish life has been created virtually from nothing in one generation.

In thinking of this incredible shift — a whole community switching continents in one generation — I realized that for the Jewish people this is not the exception but the rule: aside from the magical Holy Land of Israel, which we have always focused on and have strived to return to, we've never been permanent anywhere. When things were good, we stayed.

When things got rough, we moved. To Babylon, Persia, and Morocco. To Spain, Turkey, and India. To Germany, Poland, Russia, and America. And finally, back to Israel.

More thought revealed that there is more to the story. We didn't just move around: we profoundly affected the world, from religion to economics to culture. Numerically a small people, we were never on the sidelines: today one minor event in Israel gets more space on the front page than tragic earthquakes in India. This is not a new phenomenon: since the Jewish people have existed, we have been unique. Despised or admired, we've never been ignored. How did we make it? Why did we bother?

Those of us who have been privileged enough to receive a strong Jewish education begin to understand our history: Judaism has been for us a "portable homeland," as someone once called it. Our tradition has carried us through the centuries. It provides understanding and direction. It connects us to our grandparents, great-grandparents, and previous generations. It gives us happiness, purpose, and hope.

Yet so few of us know much about it. It has been said that more Jews know who Jesus' mother was than Moses' mother. While the comparison is a little unfair (Mary is more central to Christianity than Yocheved is to Judaism), the point is still valid.

We should know more.

Being Jewish is a wonderful inheritance. Jews today from across the spectrum of religious practice are looking to know more about their heritage. It is our hope that with this book we will begin to discover what has truly always been ours.

Doron Kornbluth

Jerusalem

5759/1999

Our People

The Chosen People

Natan Lopes Cardozo

The Chosen Claim

One of the most disturbing claims ever made by any group of people is the one Jews make when, quoting the Bible, they insist on being the "Chosen People." For nearly four thousand years, Jews have upheld the belief that they are God's elect, the "apple of His eye," His most beloved and favored nation. Superficially, this claim sounds like prejudice of the highest order, making the vast majority of mankind into second-class citizens.

Aside from Biblical references, the Jewish tradition itself has emphasized Jewish particularity and the need to build thicker walls between Jews and non-Jews. Jews are not to marry non-Jews. Judaism does not missionize or go out to win converts; rather it discourages all but the most sincere. Kosher-food laws themselves limit social interaction. Even when living amidst their non-Jewish neighbors, Jews have also always striven to live on their own, dressing differently, speaking their own language, and abiding by their own unique customs, prayers, and culture.

The famous English author George Bernard Shaw accused the Jews of arrogance and said that as long as they insisted upon their chosenness they had no right to object to the monstrous way the Germans had killed six million of their people — they had brought it on themselves. H. G. Wells called the Jewish claim "a hindrance to world unity." Protestant theologians spoke about the "haughtiness of Jewish belief."

The Universalist Claim

With all this said, it may strike us as paradoxical that traditional Judaism has gone out of its way to stress the dignity of the entire human race. When reading the Creation chapter (long before the Jews were created), we are told that all men were created in the image of God (Genesis, ch. 1). The prophet's words are clear: "Have we not all one Father; has not one God created us?" (Malachi 2:10). In Talmudic times, Rabbi Meir stated that Adam was created from dust that had been collected from all corners of the earth so that no one nation could claim the distinction of being better or having created mankind.

While not encouraging conversion, Judaism does insist that all people can become Jews. Some of the greatest Jews in history were converts or descendants of converts: The great king David comes from the line of Ruth, perhaps our most famous convert (see the Book of Ruth). Rabbi Akiva, Shemayah, and Avtalyon, some of the greatest Sages in our tradition, all traced themselves to converted forefathers. The famous commentator and Sage Onkelos was the Roman Emperor's nephew when he converted.

The Paradox

We are thus confronted with a most amazing situation.

On the one hand, we have observed how much Judaism wants to secure the Jewish people's uniqueness and chosenness. On the other hand, we are told that the equality of all men, the dignity of all human beings, is the cornerstone upon which all traditional Judaism stands.

Reality

Before trying to address this paradox, we must ask an important question: Does historical reality confirm the unique status of the Jewish people, and even its chosenness?

Our answer must be stated clearly: Yes. The cold historical facts prove that the Jewish people stand out in three matters:

1. They experienced a most miraculous survival.

2. They have made incredible contributions to civilization, totally out of proportion with their numbers.

3. They made a totally unprecedented return to their homeland after nearly two thousand years of exile.

1. Their Survival

In Biblical times, the Jews were surrounded by enemies who were committed to destroy them. They had to wage war after war to survive. Afterward they were sent into their longest exile. Beaten, killed, tortured, they were expelled from one country to another, only to find another disaster awaiting them. They became the scapegoat for national and social problems. Still, they survived. Discriminated against, consistently outlawed, the oldest nation on the planet, the Jews were constantly dying . . . yet never died. Outlasting all their enemies, they violated all the sophisticated rules of history, and for this reason became either the most annoying or the most celebrated people of the world.

2. Their Contributions

The Jewish people brought monotheism to the world, the most powerful idea man has ever heard. Since that day the universe has never been the same. The gift of the Bible turned all deeds into moral actions, teaching ethics and justice. Neither Christianity nor Islam would exist without the Jews. Based on "the Book," no international or American law would be what it is today without them. In later centuries Jews contributed to science, literature, music, finance, medicine, and art — all beyond anyone's expectations of a small, tortured people. They were involved in many social revolutions, often becoming the leaders and thinkers. They have produced great rabbis and sages, and even those who were on the road to assimilation revolutionized the world: Spinoza, Freud, Einstein, Marx.

3. The Return

Not only did the Jews manage to survive in the face of all their sufferings and make great contributions to the world, but they even managed to free themselves of their nearly two-thousand-year exile to return to the land of their forefathers. Just moments after they had experienced their worst destruction, the Holocaust, Jews picked up their bags and "went home." At a time when the whole world declared that there was no longer a future for the Jew, the State of Israel appeared — as if from nowhere. The Jewish return to their homeland was a totally unprecedented event; no nation after such a long, painful exile has successfully returned to its homeland and built a completely modern state. It is a phenomenon totally unheard of, violating all principles of conformity.

The First Jew

Having observed all this, we may confidently state that the Jews are indeed "a nation apart." Their uniqueness is beyond question, but we must ask, Does this have anything to do with the Biblical claim of chosenness? To answer this, we must turn to the Bible itself, in Genesis, chapter 11.

The generation of the Tower of Babel represented a low point in human history. They sought to build a tower high enough to reach the heavens and challenge God. For the first time, a whole generation stood up and rebelled against God as a matter of principle. While earlier generations had done much evil, they understood their actions were evil. The Tower's generation, however, brought a new ideology into the world, one of extreme secularism in which God was deliberately ignored. This new belief system saw nothing wrong with immorality — it elevated it to the new world order.

Abraham understood the inherent dangers of an ideology in which God was exiled and where immorality, corruption, and sexual depravity became the norm. He became known in the world as "Avraham the *Ivri*" (the Hebrew). *Ivri* conveys the idea of crossing a road, standing on the other side. The Jewish tradition explains: "The whole world stands on one side, and Abraham on the other." Abraham taught the world exactly what it did not want to hear: the most important thing in life is not what one has but what one is. He asked people to do that "which is just and right" (Genesis 18:19), to move toward their spiritual potential. This became the great mission of his life, of the life of his partner, Sarah, and of all his descendants.

All moral revolutions are based on this first one.

The nation that was in the process of being built was to

become the guilty conscience of the world. As Jacques Maritain remarked, "The Jews gave the world no peace, they bar slumber, they teach the world to be discontented and restless as long as the world has no God." The famous medieval commentator Seforno noted (on Exodus 19) that Abraham called for a "kingdom of priests" charged with the task of instructing and teaching the whole of mankind of the centrality of God and the importance of kindness and giving.

We can now understand more clearly our original question concerning the paradox between chosenness and universalism. The chosenness of the Jews is not a superiority-based selection at all, like that of the Nazis, who believed they were to be served by the rest of mankind. The Jews understand themselves to be the servants of mankind: a chosen messenger with a universalist message.

The particularistic aspects of the Jewish people help ensure that there will be strong messengers generation after generation. Without strong messengers there can be no strong message. Yet the goal is universal. Jews are moral protesters who understand their task as bringing the great ethical teachings of pure ethical monotheism to the entire world.

NATAN LOPES CARDOZO heads the Cardozo School for Jewish Studies and Human Dignity, a school without walls that educates young rabbis, teachers, academicians, and laypeople how to become effective ambassadors for Judaism. He is a world-renowned lecturer, known for his most original and unique insights into Judaism, through which he helps many people, Jews and non-Jews, realize the relevance of Judaism for our complicated times. He received his rabbinical degree from Gateshead Talmudic College and his doctorate in philosophy from Columbia Pacific University. He is the author of *The Torah as God's Mind* (Bepron Publications), *Between Silence and Speech* (Jason Aronson Publications), *The Infinite Chain* (Targum Press), and *The Written and Oral Torah* (Jason Aronson).

World Perfect

Ken Spiro

What would it take to make a perfect world?
If you ask almost anyone today, chances are that the answers will fall into the following six categories:

1. respect for life

2. peace and harmony between nations

3. justice and equality under the law

4. accessible education for all

5. family stability

6. social responsibility

People tend to link these values with democracy. But did they actually evolve from a democratic source?

A brief glance at the Greeks, who invented democracy, and the Romans and virtually all other ancient societies, shows us that we did not get our values from them.

Ancient Hypocrisy

1. Respect for Life

The basic right to life seems fundamental. We all want to live without fear of being arbitrarily deprived of life or dignity. As obvious and important as this seems to us to-day, however, it was not obvious or important in the ancient world.

The ancient Greeks and Romans, as well as every ancient culture we know of, practiced infanticide — the killing of newborn children as a means of population control, sex selection (boys were desired, girls not), and ridding society of burdensome or deformed members.

Babies that appeared weak or sickly at birth, or had even a minor birth defect or imperfection such as a cleft palate or harelip, were killed. This was not done by some Nazi-like baby removal squad, but by an immediate member of the family, usually the mother or father, often using methods that betray a cruelty beyond our modern imagination.

Wrote the great humanitarian Seneca: "Children . . . weak and deformed we drown, not through anger, but through wisdom, preferring the sound to the useless."

These societies also practiced human sacrifice and — when it came to the Romans — killing for entertainment. The Coliseum, and other circuses of its type, saw a level of cruelty and inhumanity beyond belief. Emperor Trajan, in the year 107 B.C.E., held games where ten thousand gladiators and three thousand wild animals fought to the death — which means thousands of human beings died — watched by spectators who ate, drank wine, and cheered the grisly spectacle.

2. Peace and Harmony

Today we understand that peace is vital to the future survival and development of humanity. Yet the Greeks and Romans built great empires by conquest. With no stigma attached even to killing for sport, killing in war wasn't worth raising an eyebrow. Indeed, the fellow who killed the most was the hero, the celebrity of his day.

3. Justice and Equality

We, who have grown up in liberal, democratic societies, realize that justice and equality are fundamental principles, that all people have the right to be treated equally under the law, regardless of who they are. But the Greek inventors of democracy didn't believe in equality. Citizens voted, but only land-owning adult males qualified as citizens. Slaves and women had no rights and could be subjugated by the power elite.

4. Education

We view free education as one of the basic responsibilities of any government toward its citizens. But in the ancient world this one ranked in the you-gotta-be-kidding category. Historians estimate that that more than 99 percent of all humanity has been illiterate. There were good reasons why education was reserved for the elite: ignorant masses are easier to control.

5. Family Stability

We appreciate today that having a stable family structure is one of the basic building blocks for a stable, healthy society. But Greek and Roman society were characterized by a disdain for women and a freewheeling obsession with sexuality. Men married women only to produce male heirs. Wrote the Greek poet Palladas: "Marriage brings a man only two happy days. The day he takes his bride to bed and the day he lays her in her grave."

The epitome of love in these ancient societies was pedastry — a sexual relationship between an older man and a young boy; today it is a very serious felony. To the Greeks this was something positive and beautiful. All the Greek greats — Sophocles, Aeschylus, and Plato, for instance — had young boy lovers. And many waxed ecstatic about it, such as the Greek poet Propertius: "May my enemies fall in love with women and my friends with boys."

Sexual promiscuity eventually had such a detrimental effect on these societies that both the Greeks and Romans eventually passed laws requiring men to marry. Yet these laws ultimately failed. When Rome collapsed in the fifth century B.C.E. it could not field an army and had to rely on mercenaries. The birth rate had plummeted, and they had no people left to fight for them. The greatest empires fell from the inside: internal rot, largely due to uncontrolled sexual behavior, helped bring about their fall.

6. Social Responsibility

Societies that did not value life, equality, or justice were not going to put much effort into social welfare programs to help those in need. No welfare checks, no soup kitchens, no food stamps. Two thousand years ago Rome, the great metropolis of 1.5 million people, the largest city on earth at the time, did not have one public hospital, asylum, or shelter.

So that is the ugly underside of Greek and Roman civilizations. This doesn't mean that all individuals were bad. Joe Average was just trying to make it through the day. But he lived in a society that had a different way of looking at the world than we do today: little regard for human life, conquest mentality, no pity for the have-nots. While they were brilliant in engineering, astronomy, literature, art, science, mathematics, and politics, these ancient societies did not produce the morality and values we cherish today.

The vision of peace, justice, and equality is not the product of ancient civilizations. There was only one small group in the ancient world that held these values: the Jews.

Jewish Values

Let's review the six fundamental values we started with:

1. Respect for Life

Abraham, the first Jew, introduced the idea of one loving God as the Creator of all. We are all God's children created in the "divine image" (Genesis 1:27). Deformed babies, slaves, women, and men — all have this divine image within them, and all have the right, therefore, to life. "Thou shalt not murder," the sixth commandment, is only one of many direct references to the infinite value of life found in the Bible.

2. Peace and Harmony

When the prophets of the Bible spoke of beating "swords into ploughshares and spears into pruning hooks" (Isaiah 2:4; Micah 4:3), they emphasized the age-old Jewish concept of universal peace and brotherhood. This vision is central to the world today, which is why these verses are inscribed on the outside of the United Nations building in New York.

3. Justice and Equality

The Bible repeats over and over that people are to be treated equally before the law: "Justice, justice you will pursue" (Deuteronomy 16:20). Setting up a fair justice system is a Biblical injunction (see Deuteronomy 16:18); accepting bribes or showing favor to the rich or powerful is clearly forbidden.

4. Education

The Jewish drive for education is almost a national obsession, and the People of the Book were enjoined in the Shema prayer itself to teach their children (ibid. 6:7). In contrast to the rest of the world, Jews have always seen education as an essential tool for improving the world and have enjoyed a unique status as history's most literate nation.

5. Family Stability

The Jewish innovation that sexuality should be confined and sanctified within the confines of marriage contributed greatly to both the stability of the family and the status of women. The Jewish people have always been known for their strong, close families. The Bible itself directs a husband to "cling unto his wife" (Genesis 2:24) and children to "respect" and "honor" their parents (fifth commandment).

6. Social Responsibility

The Jewish perspective has always been that "Love your neighbor as yourself" (Leviticus 19:19) is the basis for human interactions. The idea that we all have the moral and legal responsibility to care for others is one of Judaism's greatest innovations. The concept of *active* responsibility is the reason why the Jewish people had welfare institutions thousands of years before the rest of the world.

These were the values of the ideal society envisioned by the Bible. The greatest Jewish innovation of all is the notion of One God from Whom one standard of morality is derived — ethical monotheism. This is the revolutionary idea from which all the other great Jewish ethical innovations have come — a loving Creator Who gives His creation one standard of absolute values.

The absoluteness of the God-given standard set the Jews apart. And, indeed, for thousands of years no one much wanted to join their club. But eventually their vision and values spread worldwide. British historian Paul Johnson notes (*A History of the Jews* [Weidenfeld & Nicolson, 1987], Epilogue):

> Certainly the world without the Jews would have been a radically different place. . . . To them we owe the idea of equality before the law, both divine and human; of the sanctity of life and the dignity of the human person; of individual conscience and so of personal redemption; of the collective conscience and so of social responsibility; of peace as an abstract ideal and love as the foundation of justice, and many other items which constitute the basic moral furniture of the human mind. Without the Jews the world would have been a much emptier place. . . . It is almost beyond our capacity to imagine how the world would have fared if they had never emerged.

For two thousand years, from Abraham to the birth of Christianity, the Jewish people alone championed the notion of a just and moral world based on humanity's relationship with a loving God. Then came Christianity and Islam, both spiritual offshoots of Judaism, which converted millions of people to the belief in One God. In modern history, the greatest spreader of Jewish values outside religion has been the growth of Democracy. During the last three centuries the founding fathers of both British and especially American democracy were overwhelmingly impacted by Biblical ethics. The Bible played a central role in the curriculum of the newly founded institutions of higher learning, with both Hebrew and Bible studies being required courses. At Yale, some commencement orations were delivered in Hebrew. The Biblical education of the Founding Fathers colored their attitude toward religion and ethics — and especially politics. America was to be the new place where the old Biblical vision would take root.

Married to a Biblical standard of values, grass-roots democracy took root in America and in the last two hundred years became the fastest-spreading political system in the world. In 1800 there were three liberal democracies in the world: the United States, France, and Switzerland. In 1900 there were thirteen; in 1999, close to seventy.

So that's the story. The values held dear in modern democratic nations are largely a product of Judaism.

The mission of the Jewish people over the last 3,300 years has been to make this concept of ethical monotheism the universal vision of all humanity. This is *the* Jewish role in history and the essence of the concept of the Chosen People — a people chosen for the *responsibility* of teaching the world about one God and absolute morality.

But there is much left to do before the vision the Jewish people saw at Mount Sinai becomes a world reality. The Jews have always believed that they have a key role to play in bringing this vision to fruition. We are to create a society based on a God-given standard of morality that will serve as the model for the rest of humanity to emulate — to be "a light unto the nations."

When we look back on the vast sweep of the last four thousand years we see how significantly the Jewish people have directly and indirectly affected humanity.

The Jewish vision has become the universal vision of the world today. It is now up to the Jewish people to turn this universal vision into a reality.

KEN SPIRO is a senior researcher and lecturer at Aish HaTorah's popular Discovery seminars in Jerusalem and around the world. His master's degree and strong interest in Jewish and world history form the basis for the information in this essay, and he is the author of a soon-to-be published book on the Jewish impact on civilization.

Antisemitism and the Holocaust

Shraga Simmons

History provides far too many examples of man's inhumanity to man: social injustice, religious oppression, cultural clashes, ideological wars, class hatred, and most every other form of racism and intolerance. One particular form, however, stands out among all others: antisemitism. Unique in its universality, intensity, longevity, and irrationality, antisemitism is a historical phenomenon which falls outside of normal sociological bounds.

Historian Martin Gilbert observes in the *Jewish History Atlas*:

> As my research into Jewish history progressed, I was surprised, depressed, and to some extent overwhelmed by the perpetual and irrational violence which pursued the Jews in every country and to almost every corner of the globe. If, therefore, persecution, expulsion, torture, humiliation, and mass murder haunt these pages, it is because they also haunt the Jewish story.

Which leaves us with one question: what is the root of antisemitism?

"Jews Are Rich, Powerful, and Control the World"

Many claim that antisemitism is a reaction to Jewish political and economic power. Consider *The Protocols of the Elders of Zion*, a book invented by the Russian secret police purporting to be the discussions of Jewish elders plotting to take over the world. It was — next to the Bible — the best-selling book in the world during the 1920s. In the United States, Henry Ford sponsored its publication. It has since been printed in numerous languages internationally and presently has widespread distribution in Japan.

But could Jewish wealth and power be the cause of antisemitism? The Jews of Poland and Russia were poor and powerless, yet they were still persecuted. Cossacks didn't check bank accounts before initiating pogroms. When the Nazis liquidated the Warsaw ghetto, the Jews lived there under incredibly impoverished conditions. The reality is that poor Jews have been just as hated as rich Jews.

Jewish success may make an antisemite gnash his teeth, but it's clearly not the root cause of antisemitism.

"Jews Claim to Be the Chosen People"

The University of California at Berkeley conducted a survey, asking a group of non-Jewish Americans whether they believed a series of negative statements about Jews. By far the number one belief (held by 59 percent) was that Jews consider themselves God's chosen people.

It is true that Jews have always claimed to be different. Throughout history, Jews have maintained a completely different ethical, cultural, and social system — including different, dress, laws, and language. To top it all off, Jewish allegiance was never primarily to the countries in which they lived. The Jew always dreamed of going back to Zion. They were the ultimate outsiders.

If antisemites hate us because we claim to be chosen, what happens when Jews drop their claim of chosenness? When the Enlightenment came to Europe, many Jews said, "Now's our chance!" They shed their foreign dress, shaved their beards, enrolled in universities, and intermarried. In Germany and Austria, Jews for the first time said, "We're no longer chosen. We're going to become like you. Our home is here. Berlin is our Jerusalem." After centuries of hatred, the Jews anticipated a warm welcome from their gentile neighbors. Yet where do we see the most vicious outpouring of antisemitism in all of history? Precisely in Germany and Austria — at the time and place where Jews dropped the claim of chosenness!

Other reasons have been suggested for antisemitism, but they are also lacking. Some say Jews were a convenient scapegoat — but hatred must exist as a precondition to be chosen as a scapegoat (e.g., no one ever chose the disabled as the scapegoat for a country's problems).

Others suggest that antisemitism exists because of deicide: we killed their god. But historians show that antisemitism existed before Christianity and has appeared in countless non-Christian countries.

We can see, then, that all the stated reasons are not reasons at all, but rather are excuses for antisemitism. What is the real reason?

The Attempt to De-Judaize Antisemitism

In her diary, on April 11, 1944, Anne Frank wrote:

Who has made us Jews different from all other people?
Who has allowed us to suffer so terribly up till now? It
is God Who has made us as we are, but it will be God,
too, Who will raise us up again. *Who knows, it might
even be our religion from which the world and all peoples
learn good, and for that reason, and that reason only, do
we now suffer* [emphasis mine]. We can never become
just Netherlanders or just English or representatives of
any country, for that matter. We will always remain
Jews.

Anne Frank said, in effect, that Jews have something
special to contribute to the world, and because of that we
have been persecuted.

But by and large, the world would rather de-Judaize antisemitism. When *The Diary of Anne Frank* was adapted into a
Broadway play, we hear her explanation of antisemitism
quite differently:

"Why are Jews hated?" she asks. "Well, one day it's
one group and the next day another. . . ."

In other words, the reasons for antisemitism have absolutely nothing to do with being Jewish. The Jews went
through a Holocaust, the most systematic attempt to murder a people in the history of all humanity — and it was not
for Jewish reasons. Dumb luck. We were simply in the wrong
place at the wrong time.

Hitler's Reason for Antisemitism

There was one individual, however, who stated clearly
that hatred of Jews is because there's something unique
about the Jews. Adolf Hitler. His driving ambition was to
turn the world away from monotheism and bring it back to

paganism. He stood for the superiority of the Aryan race: "Might makes right. . . . Survival of the fittest . . . eliminate the infirm and handicapped."

There was only one obstacle standing in Hitler's way: the Jews. Hitler knew it was the Jews who introduced to humanity the ideas of love your neighbor, helping the poor and sick, and all men are created equal. Hitler hated the message of the Jews because it totally contradicted what he wanted the world to become.

As Hitler said:

> Providence has ordained that I should be the greatest liberator of humanity. I am freeing man from the restraints of an intelligence that has taken charge, from the dirty and degrading self-mortifications of a false vision called conscience and morality, and from the demands of a freedom and personal independence which only a very few can bear.

and

> The Ten Commandments have lost their validity. Conscience is a Jewish invention; it is a blemish like circumcision.

Hitler's antisemitism was not a means to an end. It was his goal.

With the Nazi invasion of Hungary in 1944, top German military officers determined that railway lines must be used to transport vital troops and equipment to the battle front. The Wehrmacht urged Hitler to provide this infusion of desperately needed supplies. Ignoring their warnings, Hitler instead gave orders to allocate the precious rail lines to deport hundreds of thousands of Hungarian Jews en masse to the extermination camps. Historians acknowledge this decision as a key factor in further debilitating the German war effort. Hitler, it seems, regarded the killing of Jews as even more important than winning World War II.

He said:

> If only one country, for whatever reason, tolerates a Jewish family in it, that family will become the germ center for fresh sedition. If one little Jewish boy survives, without any Jewish education, with no synagogue and no Hebrew school, it's in his soul.

The Torah View of Antisemitism

The Torah itself teaches that antisemitism will exist and that Jews will be hated for precisely the reasons echoed in Hitler's words.

The Talmud (*Shabbos* 69) declares:

> Why was the Torah given on a mountain called "Sinai"? Because the great *sinah*, the great hatred of the Jew, emanates from Sinai. [*Sinah*, the Hebrew word for "hatred," is pronounced almost identically to *Sinai*.]

Before the Torah was given, people built their lives on a subjective concept of right and wrong. At Sinai the Jewish people were told there is one God for all humanity Who makes moral demands on human beings. You can't just live as you please; there is a higher authority to whom you are accountable.

The Jews were given the responsibility to represent that morality and be a "light unto the nations." So, despite the fact that they were never more than a tiny fraction of the world's population, Jewish ideas became the basis for the civilized world. And with that, they became a lightning rod for those opposed to the moral message. That's why the Russians, although they were a huge superpower in the 1970s, were threatened by a handful of Jews who wanted to study Hebrew.

Why would people hate the Jewish message?

Consider the words of Aldous Huxley in his book *Confessions of an Atheist*:

> I had motives for not wanting the world to have meaning; consequently, I assumed that it had none and was able without difficulty to find satisfying reasons for this assumption. For myself, as no doubt for most of my contemporaries, the philosophy of meaninglessness was essentially an instrument of liberation. The liberation we desired was simultaneously liberation from a certain political and economic system and liberation from a certain system of morality. *We objected to the morality because it interfered with our sexual freedom* [emphasis mine].

The Holocaust showed us that for the one who rejects morality and conscience, the only way to get rid of the message is to destroy the messenger.

Why Be Jewish?

The solution to antisemitism is the flip side of the cause. Jewish values are the cause of antisemitism, and Jewish values are the solution. Only by studying Torah — and teaching it to others — can we ever hope to bring the world to a point where evil is eradicated.

When human beings embrace the moral doctrine Judaism brought to the world from Sinai — that there is a God

Who demands ethical behavior from every human being —
then there will be no holocausts.

And that is the exquisite irony of Jewish history.

The world cannot get the message unless the messengers learn it and teach it. The world desperately needs the Jewish message. Now go and study.

SHRAGA SIMMONS spent his childhood trekking through snow in Buffalo, New York. With a background in journalism and rabbinics, he is now editor of the Aish HaTorah Web site (www.aish.edu).

References:

Prager, Dennis, and Joseph Telushkin. *Why the Jews?*

Rausching, Herman. *Hitler Speaks.*

Shore, Raphael. "Why the Jews?" Seminar. Aish HaTorah.

Why Jews Can't Be for Jesus

Michael Skobac

Jewish people today are the focus of a massive, concerted effort by evangelical Christians to win our souls to their faith. There are hundreds of organizations today spending huge sums of money to aggressively target Jewish communities worldwide. Many of these groups camouflage their activities with a Jewish veneer. They refer to the Christian faith as "Messianic Judaism," to their clergy as "rabbis," and to their churches as "synagogues." They adopt and pervert traditional Jewish symbols and holidays to make potential converts lower their guard and to dampen the guilt of conversion. One of the primary goals of these missionaries is to convince Jewish people that embracing Jesus as the Messiah does not contradict Jewish teachings.

YOU'RE A TWAHOOSEY!

No, I'm not.

Yes, you are.

No, I'm not.

Yes, you are.

There is only one way to solve this dispute: look in the dictionary to see what a twahoosey is and then look at the candidate — does he or she fit the definition?

Same thing with claiming someone is the Jewish Messiah: before we can evaluate anyone's claim to being the Messiah, we must (1) have a clear working definition of what the Messiah is and (2) see if our candidate fits the definition. This point needs to be stressed, because the Christian case for Jesus usually works backwards. They assume from the outset that Jesus was the Messiah and then search for Biblical quotes to support that position.

The Biblical Portrait of the Messiah

The word *messiah* is a rendering into English of the Hebrew word *mashiach*, which means "anointed." In the Bible, special personalities in the service of God, such as kings, high priests, and prophets, are referred to as "anointed ones" or "messiahs." For example, David explains why he wouldn't harm King Saul, who was pursuing him, by saying:

> God forbid that I should do this thing to my master, God's anointed one [messiah], to raise my hand against him, for he is God's messiah.

(I Samuel 24:6)

When David later becomes king, he is also referred to as God's anointed one or messiah (II Samuel 23:1).

Interestingly, there is no direct reference in the Bible to any future personality who is to be called "the Messiah." We must therefore clearly understand where the concept of the Messiah can be found in the Bible.

Messianic Prophecies

Some Biblical prophecies are calls to correct our ways and return to deeper relationships with God. Other Biblical prophecies are futuristic, and their central theme refers to an ultimate age of perfection characterized by universal peace and knowledge of God. The focus of this utopian picture is on the restoration of the Jewish people to their homeland, where they will live in peace and serve as a spiritual beacon to the world. This vision is developed through hundreds of references in the Bible (set A) such as:

> And it will come to pass that in the end of days the mountain of the house of God will be established as the highest of the mountains and raised up above the hills and peoples will stream to it. Many nations will go and say, "Come, let us go up to the mountain of God, to the house of the God of Jacob, and He will teach us His ways and we will walk in His paths." For out of Zion shall the Torah go forth, and the word of God from Jerusalem. He will judge between many peoples, and arbitrate between nations far away. They will beat their swords into plowshares, and their spears into pruning hooks. Nation shall not lift up sword against nation, nor shall they learn war anymore. But they shall all sit under their own vines and under their own fig trees, and no one shall make them afraid, for the mouth of the God of Hosts has spoken.

> *(Micah 4:1–4)*

A number of these passages (subset B) speak of a righteous descendant of King David who will rule Israel during this transformed age:

"The days are surely coming," says God, "when I will fulfill the promise I made to the house of Israel and to the house of Judah. In those days and at that time, I will cause a righteous sprout to spring forth from David, and he shall execute justice and righteousness in the land. In those days, Judah will be safe, and Jerusalem will dwell securely. And this is the name by which it will be called: 'God is our righteousness.'"

(Jeremiah 33:14–16)

(A similar passage in Jeremiah 23:5–6 makes it clear that this person will rule Israel as king. See also Isaiah 11:1–9, 30:7–9; Ezekiel 34:23–31, 37:24–28; Hosea 3:4–5; Zechariah 9:9–10; II Samuel 7:12–13 et. al.)

By convention, we refer to this future king who will rule over a restored Israel in a transformed world as "the Messiah."

Significantly, there is no other information about a future anointed one from the line of David in the Bible. The Bible only gives *one* definition of the Messiah: he is to be the acknowledged leader of the Jewish people during the world's utopian age. Because the world has not yet reached its utopian perfection (read the newspaper for proof), it is clear the Messiah has not yet come. Whoever Jesus was, he was not, could not have been, the Messiah: he didn't lead the Jewish people, and even now, two thousand years later, we still haven't entered the utopian age.

Clear Passages and Vague Passages

It is important to understand that the messianic prophetic theme is developed clearly and consistently throughout the Bible. By clear we mean that the passages are straightforward and unambiguous, with universal agreement to their meaning. Even Christian readers of the Bible readily admit that the passages we have cited clearly refer to the Messiah and to the Messianic Age. By consistenT, we mean that the concept is not based on a few isolated references, but is developed organically throughout the Bible.

This same degree of clarity does not apply to virtually any of the passages that Christians have historically cited as "proof texts" that Jesus was the Messiah (set C). Verses such as "The stone that the builders rejected has become the chief cornerstone" (Psalms 118:22) or "Even my close friend, who I trusted, who ate of my bread, has lifted up his heel against 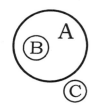 me" (ibid. 41:10) could only be seen as Messianic allusions by those searching for verses in the Bible that bear some resemblance to Jesus. Anyone reading the Bible before Christianity would not have assumed that these verses were describing the Messiah. The out-of-context use of those "proof" texts by missionaries employs circular reasoning — similar to the parable where the archer first shoots his arrows into the tree and then draws a target around them. The ambiguity of these passages is evident in that even Christian scholars themselves dispute their meaning. Proof is only possible when there is no question about what a passage means — something that can mean anything means nothing.

Conclusion

We started this essay by saying that there are only two ways to know if you are a twahoosey: (1) get the definition and (2) see if it applies. Same thing for the Messiah: (1) clear unambiguous verses describe the Messiah as the leader of the Jewish people in the utopian age of humankind, and (2) Jesus did not fit the bill. We added that Christian "proof" texts are inevitably vague and ambiguous: there is no proof that they refer to Jesus or to the Messiah.

With a clear understanding of what the Messiah is, it is impossible to claim that Jesus was the Jewish Messiah, and to do so goes completely against Jewish tradition and the Bible itself.

MICHAEL SKOBAC is senior counselor and educational director of Jews for Judaism, an international countermissionary, counseling, and educational network dedicated to countering the multimillion dollar efforts of missionary and cult groups that target the Jewish community for conversion. He has specialized in countermissionary work since 1983 and has lectured, counseled, and consulted around the world on missionary and cult issues. A columnist for the *Jewish Press*, he has appeared on many radio and television programs to discuss his work.

Our Life

A British Officer in India

Judy Auerbach

I was participating in a V.I.S.A. Shabbaton (Shabbat program) in the scenic city of Safed, Israel. Along with all the other students I was singing and dancing, studying, talking, walking, hiking, enjoying, when I realized how much I loved being Jewish. Spending my junior year of college in Israel, I'd discovered Judaism's beauty, its depth, its flavor. I was so grateful to have come here.

The way I got to Israel was through a college exchange program, but the reason I came was to explore Judaism, to find out what it offered, to understand life, to reconnect with my religion, my history, my homeland. Someone told me that the Talmud says the air of Israel makes a person wise, and I believe it. It has worked for me. The Jewish people were forced out of their land against their will, and over the centuries they never stopped trying to come back. They prayed in the direction of Jerusalem, and in their prayers three times a day they asked to return. At Passover they said, "*L'shanah haba'ah biYerushalyim* — Next year in Jerusalem." No wonder there are so many places to study, learn, and explore — there is no place like it. The land is part of us.

It was in this wonderful atmosphere that I came to hear

of an idea that changed me permanently. I'd heard the idea before, but I guess I wasn't ready for it yet. Someone on the Shabbaton recommended a book she had read and even wrote down the title and author for me. It was a *New York Times* bestseller, she said. I asked around and finally found a copy to borrow. The book was called *The Closing of the American Mind* by Professor Allan Bloom of the University of Chicago (Simon & Schuster, 1988). To be honest, the last part dealt with German philosophy which was a little above me, but no matter. One experience he shared will remain permanently etched in my mind.

I haven't seen it in a while, but this is the gist of it. He had taught philosophy for years, and every year he asked his freshmen students what they would do in the following situation: You are a British colonel in service to Her Majesty's army in India before they got independence there. You are touring the countryside when you notice a huge procession, sobbing and screaming. Quickly you realize it is a funeral procession. It seems a young man died tragically, and the whole village is attending the ceremony. Then you notice a young woman being led along, and there are two big stacks of wood waiting at the front. One will be used to burn his dead body, as is the custom here. The other is to burn the widow's live body — as is the custom here. Then the professor would ask, "What do you do? Do you stop it? Do you want to stop it?" He would always get answers such as "The British shouldn't have been there in the first place" or "It wasn't their country. What gives them the right to come here and tell others what to do?"

It seemed tolerance of other cultures and mutual respect had gone so far as to convince American students that there were no absolute rights and wrongs. Professor Bloom would declare himself an absolutist: There are some things that are absolutely, positively wrong, and I don't care whose culture is doing them. Murdering a healthy woman just because her husband died is simply wrong. His students would look at him as if he were a Martian. The concept that "I do what I want, and you do what you want; you don't tell me how to live, and I don't tell you how to live" had been pounded into their psyches consciously and subconsciously through school and the media. They had been taught (as had I, which is why the idea so affected me) that everything was relative. I had always thought that what is right for me is right for me, and what is right for you is right for you. It had never occurred to me that some rules might apply to both of us.

The first time I visited the Western Wall in Jerusalem I heard the same idea. My tour guide sat us down somewhere and suggested that we find a few minutes to be alone. No cameras, no sharing impressions, no distractions. Just be alone and completely quiet. This was hard for us, who grew up with computers, televisions, answering machines, radios — we were not used to quiet. We were to close our eyes and look into ourselves. Our guide assured us that we would discover that inside we *did* believe there was meaning to life.

He had suggested this exercise to connect us to the meaning of the Wall. When I finally let myself do it (it took a while, I admit), it meant even more to me. While I can't prove anything to anybody, there are certain things I *know* are wrong, and I can say that with utmost certainty. In speaking with many people about this, I think everyone believes this if they are honest with themselves. There is meaning. There are things that are just right and things that are just wrong.

Your objections can already be heard: Hitler! Stalin! Pol Pot! The Crusades! Look at what the idea of absolute truth has done to the world. Wars have been fought, millions of innocent people have died, the world has been ravaged, all because of the idea that "what I believe is right; what you believe is wrong." My only answer is to say that *how* you deal with the truth is a separate subject (tolerance vs. forcing others to accept your beliefs), as is *how* you figure out which truths are really true (to me it is clear that murdering a widow just because her husband died is simply wrong, no if's, and's, or but's) and which are not (for example, millions once felt that it was an absolute truth that the Earth was flat, which we know now to have been a mistake). Both of those are important but separate subjects — what I am discussing is the simple idea that everything is not relative, that absolute truth does exist. My point can be summed up as follows: don't believe everything you hear; real truth is not relative.

There. That is all I wanted to share. It is a simple idea, and I didn't want to take too much space explaining it. It took me being in the beautiful Land of Israel for the idea to sink in, but I think it is important that everyone hear it no matter where they are.

See you at the Wall!

Editor's note: the Visiting Israel Students' Association (V.I.S.A.) is a popular nonprofit organization that provides young Jews visiting Israel with the opportunity to explore and enjoy Judaism.

JUDY AUERBACH is a pseudonym for a writer presently living in Jerusalem.

Disconnecting Myself

Rivkah Slonim

New friends are puzzled, even dismayed, when they hear about the way I observe Shabbat. They are bewildered to learn that I do not write, flip an electric switch, use the telephone, cook, or engage in a host of assorted everyday activities for twenty-five hours each week, starting Friday night at sunset until Saturday at nightfall. After that brief pocket in time, I am back, rushing to the same beat we all recognize. No one who sees me in the throes of the hurry which defines my life would ever believe I take such a prolonged hiatus on such a regular basis. How can you afford to do that? they ask. When they hear that my observance also precludes shopping, theater-going, and a wide gamut of recreational activities, the question turns shrill: Why would you *want* to do that?

This line of questioning is not at all surprising. It flows quite naturally from the assumption that to cease from our everyday pursuits on a regular basis is not only difficult but impossible. Think of the advertisements we see of the mountain climber perched precariously as he logs on with his laptop to check his mail, or the sunbather on a remote island clinching a deal in communication with the office.

Now think again, this time of the advertisements for

the Club Med vacation options, those coveted holiday pack-
ages for the rich and elite. What distinguishes these get-
aways from all others is more than the lusciousness of the
remote islands, the exotic food and entertainment or extrav-
agant accommodations. It is the utter removal they offer
from the everyday din and commotion. The plug is pulled on
phones, fax, and e-mail. What a phenomenon! And that's
what I experience each week when on Friday, just as the sun
is about to set, I disconnect myself from the everyday sum-
monses. I light the Shabbat candles, and something changes
as I clear my mind of the craziness of the week and take a
deep breath. I know I am in a place to which I could never
have arrived on my own.

Six Days of Work

The fourth of the Ten Commandments states:

> Remember the Sabbath to keep it holy. You shall work
> during the six weekdays and do all your tasks. But Sat-
> urday is the Sabbath to God your Lord. Do not do any-
> thing that constitutes work.

> (Exodus 20:8–10)

There is an indication here that resting on Shabbat is in-
trinsically connected to, even contingent upon, the work we
do during the week. To understand the nature of man's work
we go back to the beginning, even before Genesis.

God created this world, we are taught, to fulfill His
deepest desire. More than anything else, God wanted that
there exist beings who would, of their own choice, recognize
Him and adhere to His commandments. To do this, God had
to create a being who could in every way feel independent

and unconstrained. The description of man's formation appears rather simple: God fashioned a form from the earth and then breathed life into it. The result, however, was complex. The name *Adam* is reflective of an unlikely synergy; *Adam* is on the one hand linked to the Biblical word *adamah*, "earth," and on the other to the concept of *adameh l'elyon*, "in God's likeness." The mundane and the sublime, the earthy and the spiritual, the temporal and the celestial. It is in this dialectic that we begin to understand the species known as man.

God spent six days creating a stage on which we are all the actors. He did this by concealing Himself — in Kabbalistic terms, contracting His energy and pulling back, thus creating an "empty place," a place in which He was not overtly manifest, a place we call "the world." The Hebrew word for "world," *olam*, is etymologically rooted in *he'elem*, "shrouded and obscured." God remains hidden to allow us our freedom, our ability to choose. Our mandate? *L'takein olam*, to perfect the world, uplift it, invest it with goodness and spirituality. In essence, it is an exercise in the process of revelation: to unmask the Godliness inherent in this world.

Shabbat: A Time to Return

It is obvious that we cannot accomplish our mission by removing ourselves from the world. It is only by working within this physical, material realm that we can uncover the Godly sparks contained therein. The very nature of this exercise, however, is fraught with danger. As we become submerged in this world, we must struggle to remain above it. In the endless tension between earth and spirit, sheer weight often wins out. It is easy to forget our source, our reason for being, our point of departure and return for this journey we call life. Shabbat is a potent reminder; it takes us back to the beginning.

The first two letters of the Hebrew word *shabbat* form the word *shav*, "return." Shabbat is a time of reunion, a return to the unity our soul enjoyed with God before being sent into its present existence. It is a return also to the perfection that existed after the six days of Creation, before sin and the ensuing disruption. Because of the "earthiness" of our existence, we need to be nudged into this return. It is for this reason that God commands us to "remember the seventh day and make it holy." This, God tells us, can be accomplished only through rest.

Shabbat: A Day of Rest

What is considered rest? It is facile and confusing to state that on Shabbat we stop working. Most of us know very observant Jews who "work" hard on Saturdays. They might be rabbis or cantors or neighbors down the block who open their homes to streams of guests with whom they share Shabbat meals. They don't seem to be resting! Just as perplexing are the many acts prohibited under the rubric of work that are not tiring or laborious at all.

It is necessary to understand the notion of work as it applies uniquely to Shabbat. Rabbi Samson Raphael Hirsch defined it: an activity is deemed work and thus a forbidden action on Shabbat based on its creative dimension. Simply put, on Shabbat we are commanded to cease from all behavior which leads to the creation of something new in this physical world (spiritual and intellectual growth and innovation is not curtailed; i.e., one may compose a melody or write a new poem in one's mind).

On Shabbat we desist from harnessing this world's energies and forces. We suspend our ongoing efforts to maste and transform our environment. For this reason the simple action of flipping a switch, which creates an electric current, is prohibited on Shabbat, while dragging a heavy sofa across the house for the purpose of seating extra people is not. In one, we are engaging a force outside ourselves to create a new situation; in the other, we are merely expending our energy on moving something, but its essential nature remains the same. Similarly, we may not cook raw food, changing its state through the application of heat, but we can serve as many guests as we like. In like manner, we may not open an umbrella, creating a form of shelter, but we may tidy all the beds in our home.

In mirroring God's original pattern we cease, after six days of invention and innovation, from all forms of creation in the material realm. In that suspension of our power and prowess, we lift the veil and come face to face with our God, with our selves, and with our reason for being.

Shabbat: A Time of Sensory Delight

Shabbat is marked by a deep, sweet, peaceful tempo, a cadence all its own. And it is filled with unique purpose and activity. We spend time with family and friends. Our prayers are unhurried. Our minds are calmer and more open to study or quiet contemplation. Simply put, Shabbat affords us the opportunity to take a deep breath and reflect on our week, much like an artist who might take a step back to look at an unfinished painting and ponder its strengths and deficiencies.

And Shabbat is a time of material, corporeal pleasure. In observant homes, even the two-year-olds know that on Shabbat they get to wear their special Shabbat clothes and shoes, their fanciest hair bow or tie. The ten-year-olds know there will be extra treats, not to mention more time with Mom and Dad. The adults know there will be wonderful meals, and the house will be freshly cleaned, with everyone carefully groomed and dressed in their finest. The table will be beautifully set, maybe even accented by fresh flowers; the Shabbat candles will cast their magic glow.

Upon reflection, this all sounds rather strange. If Shabbat is about remembering God's omniscience and omnipotence, why squander the celestial on temporal pleasures?

The simple answer is that on Shabbat it is a mitzvah to experience delight and pleasure, for in doing so we mirror the joy and contentment experienced by God after the six days of Creation. On the deepest level, however, we understand this by going back to the rest and work relationship we spoke of earlier. During the week, our charge is to act in partnership with God by perfecting this world. We are engaged in looking beyond the plurality that confronts us to localize the unifying factor, the essence, the Godly spark. This is difficult, laborious work. The material world and mindset is generally resistant to our overtures. On Shabbat, however, we rest. That is, there is no longer the tension between the physical and spiritual, for everything is more manifestly an expression of God. Even in the most physical actions — in our eating and drinking — we perceive that we are involved in holy pursuit.

Tradition has it that on Friday nights angels visit each Jewish home. They are welcomed with the singing of a hymn called *"Shalom Aleichem."* Oddly enough, the first stanzas of welcome and our request for their blessing is followed quickly by bidding them goodbye:

Welcome, O angels of peace. . . . Come in peace. . . .
Bless us in peace. . . . Take leave in peace. . . .

Why, instead of asking the angels to grace our home
with their presence, do we seem to hurry them out? Why
don't we ask them to stay with us for the duration of our
meal and celebration?

Jewish mysticism teaches that the angels, much as
they might want to stay, simply cannot tolerate the experience. Upon their entrance into a Jewish home that has accepted the Shabbat, they are blinded and overwhelmed by a
Godly light so luminous that they must flee! The light of
Shabbat far surpasses anything angels experience in heaven,
for it is the fire created by our adherence to God's command,
the glow generated by our choice, the torch of combined
sparks we have freed, the light for which the entire world
was created. And it is ours to bask in — on Shabbat.

RIVKAH SLONIM is education director of the Chabad House
Jewish Student Center in Binghamton, New York, and an internationally known teacher, lecturer, and activist with a special focus
on women in Jewish law and life. She is the author of the ac-
claimed book *Total Immersion: A Mikvah Anthology* (Jason
Aronson, 1996) and a consultant to educators on the subject of
mikveh and Jewish family life.

The Wonder of Torah Study

Eli Gewirtz

It is considered normal, at least in the academic world, to major in a particular discipline and dedicate much of one's study time to subjects that relate to its central theme.

Then you graduate.

Except for a select group of budding academics, the vast majority move on. Sure, they'll read a book here and there and occasionally take various "continuing education" classes. But essentially they get on with life. Even researchers and academics don't spend their down time reviewing material they've already mastered.

Not so Jews studying their tradition. We read, study, and reread the weekly Torah portion. One year later, when the Torah- reading cycle is complete, we read, study, and reread the same portions over again. After studying a volume, or even one chapter of the Talmud, we say, "*Hadran alach* — We'll return to you." We may be moving on for now, but hang in there, we're coming back.

Does it take Jews longer for it to sink in? Why do accomplished Torah scholars constantly review material they supposedly mastered twenty-five years earlier?

A deeper look at Torah study reveals that it is a subject

like no other. Of course, some components are predictable. We must, for example, study and review the law to know what and how to observe. But there's more to it than that.

To help us better understand what Torah study is all about, it is necessary to present a few basic premises.

Torah is the expression of God's will.

We sometimes forget that Torah is the word of God — an instruction manual for how to achieve the most out of life, the verbal embodiment of God Himself. By studying the Torah, we are actually in a process of bonding with God. This concept may be difficult, especially for the uninitiated. But most people believe that we each have a soul. Jewish tradition teaches us that the soul yearns for a connection with its Source, God. Torah study provides that connection.

Torah study provides an important tool for life: critical thinking.

In Jewish parlance, the words *truth* and *Torah* are synonymous. If it ain't true, it ain't Torah. We are expected to not only *live* that truth, but to actively *experience* it. While a passive review of the *Shulchan Aruch* (a compilation of Jewish law, absent the Talmudic give-and-take) would adequately furnish the details of Torah law, we are enjoined to examine the sources ourselves in the original. As we review the sources, it is likely we will encounter conflicting opinions and statements. It is the very analysis of these seemingly irreconcilable contradictions that helps clarify the truth and intensifies our overall understanding of the subject matter.

Torah study provides another important tool for life: intellectual honesty.

Most people go through life holding on to old opinions and attitudes for dear life. Young racists become old racists, Democrats remain Democrats, Republicans remain Republicans. Nobody wants their foundation rattled. Intellectually honest people, however, are excited and ready for a challenge. If given solid evidence contrary to a held assumption, they'll adopt a new approach. Torah study, especially when done together with a *chavruta* (study partner), helps develop this essential tool. It's easy to misinterpret a particular verse or some Talmudic passage. But the analysis of an individual verse or passage is almost never done in isolation. It has to jive with all the other references. When you realize it doesn't, you are forced to step back and rethink. This process of examining, debating, and then reexamining previously held assumptions is the meat and potatoes of Torah study.

Finally, *Torah study has a rather unique effect, especially on its more industrious students.* It simultaneously challenges the mind, brings joy to the heart, stimulates the intellect, and uplifts the spirit. The process of resolving a seemingly irreconcilable discrepancy or of arriving at a text's deeper meaning results in a sense of joy and fulfillment that is unparalleled in any other academic pursuit.

Okay, Torah study is good for the Jews. But how much is necessary? If devoting, say, a half-hour a day is enough, why do many Jews devote several hours each day? And if it really takes hours, should someone who can only spare moments a day even bother?

The answer can be gleaned from a Talmudic statement regarding a Sage known as Rav Idi. Rav Idi would travel for a full three months in order to spend one day studying at a renowned yeshivah. That's right, one day. After the day was up, he'd pick himself up, make an about-face, and commence his three-month journey back home. From what I know about yeshivot, it probably wasn't the food that made the trip worthwhile. We can also surmise that, after three months of travel, he was probably exhausted.

Was it worth it? To Rav Idi it obviously was. By describing Rav Idi's journey, the Talmud is teaching us that quality, more than quantity, is what counts. Sure, Rav Idi could have studied elsewhere and easily cover more textual ground. But he knew about something special available only in the environment of that yeshivah and recognized that one day of it was clearly worth the six-month trip. We can thus infer that the Torah study of someone who can only afford to set aside a small portion of his or her day is potentially as valuable as that of someone else who can devote more time. If Rav Idi had more time, we can be sure he'd have stayed longer. But if a small amount of time is all you've got, its value is potentially as great, or possibly greater, than someone who puts in more time.

Indeed, we are taught about the importance of designating a specific time, even a small amount, for Torah study. Let this serve as your invitation to join the ranks of college students, doctors, lawyers, carpenters, and businesspeople who part company from their busy schedules for a quick dip into the vast sea of Jewish learning. Come on in, the water's fine.

ELI GEWIRTZ is the director of Partners in Torah, a nationwide Jewish learning network offering free one-to-one tutorial study, either in person or over the phone, on any topic. Free phone cards are provided for long-distance study. Call 1-800-STUDY-4-2.

Brain Food:
The Jewish Dietary Laws

Mordechai Becher

Few activities are as instinctive as eating, and few activities have such a profound impact on us physiologically, psychologically, and spiritually. Many people do not give much thought to when, what, and how they eat until their cardiologist tells them to lower their cholesterol or their friends begin to ask if they are pregnant (for men this question is especially disturbing). Jews who observe the dietary laws (kashrut), however, must make regular decisions about what they eat, when they eat it, and how they prepare their food. For the observant Jew eating ceases to be a totally instinctive activity. The dietary laws force us to stop and think about daily activities and deter us from going through life in autopilot.

In order to understand what the Torah wants us focus on, and to understand the philosophy of kashrut, it is necessary to be superficially familiar with the kashrut laws themselves. Following is a brief overview:

- A kosher animal must be a ruminant (a cud-chewing animal) and have split hooves. Cows, sheep, goats, and deer are all kosher, whereas camels and pigs (

having each only one sign of kashrut) are not. Most common fowl, such as chickens, ducks, and geese, are kosher, but the birds of prey (hawks, eagles, etc.) are not kosher. A sea creature is only kosher if it has fins and scales, so most species of fish are kosher (tuna, salmon, flounder, etc.), but all shellfish are not kosher; dolphins, whales, and squids are also not kosher. Any food product of a non-kosher animal is also non-kosher. The exception to this rule is bee's honey.

- An animal or bird must be slaughtered according to Jewish law. This involves cutting the animal's trachea and esophagus (the carotid and jugular are also severed) with a surgically sharp knife. The cut must be swift, continuous, and performed by an expert. This method of slaughter reduces the blood pressure in the brain to zero immediately, so the animal loses consciousness in a few seconds and dies in minutes.

- The animal or bird must be free of *treifot*, which are seventy different categories of injuries, diseases, or abnormalities whose presence renders the animal non-kosher.

- Certain fats, known as *cheilev*, may not be eaten. Blood must be removed from the meat, either by soaking, salting, and rinsing or by broiling. The sciatic nerve in each leg and the surrounding fat must be removed.

- It is forbidden to cook, eat, or benefit from milk and meat mixtures. It is also forbidden to cook or eat dairy products together with poultry.

- In Israel, tithes must be taken from all crops. If these tithes are not separated, then the produce may not be eaten — the wheat, barley, or fruit is actually not kosher until the commandments of tithing have been fulfilled.

- Milk products (including the rennet in cheese) must only come from kosher animals.

The most obvious idea behind kashrut is self-control and discipline. Let me illustrate this with a real-life example.

Most parents are familiar with the horrors of going to the supermarket with young children. The worst part of this ordeal is waiting in line at the checkout counter. You have only five items, so you wait in the "eight items or less" express line. The lady in front of you has twenty-five items at least, she is trying to pay with a third-party check from Paraguay in Thai baht, and she is negotiating with the clerk over her expired coupons (and her mortgage). You are waiting with two children under the age of six surrounded on both sides by four-foot high walls of sugar-based products. The children are becoming increasingly impatient and begging for candies, and you are becoming more angry and frustrated as time goes on. Of course, most children will scream, beg, and embarrass their parents into buying the candy.

Now for the true story. I moved with my family from Israel to Toronto for a four-year stay and in the first week was waiting in line at the supermarket with one of my children. He asked me for a chocolate bar. I looked at the bar and told him it was not kosher. He was silent, accepting the decision without tantrums, threats, tears, or hysteria. It struck me then that my five-year-old, who has been brought up with the laws of kashrut, had more self-control than millions of adults in the Western world. How many people accept no as an answer in denial of a pleasure that they want *now*? Dangerous? I will take precautions. Unhealthy? I will stop after a few. Addictive? Not to me. Not to indulge is simply not an option.

In Jewish tradition we are allowed to use animals as food and clothing. However, we are not supposed to rejoice in this, and we are certainly not supposed to make a sport of it. Some laws of kashrut are designed to prevent us from becoming callous and cruel and to discourage hunting as a form of recreation or sustenance. The requirements of *shechitah* (slaughtering) and *treifot* virtually preclude the possibility of hunting. In the words of a great rabbi:

> I am amazed by this activity [hunting]. We have not found hunters in the Torah except for Nimrod and Esau. This is not the way of the sons of Abraham, Isaac, and Jacob. . . . It is written, "His mercy is upon all his creatures.". . . If so, how can an Israelite kill living beings without any other need than in order to pass his time by hunting? . . . This matter contributes to cruelty and is forbidden. . . .

The prohibition against meat and milk also serves to remind us where our food comes from. The meat is from a dead animal, the milk from a living animal. Be aware that obtaining meat necessitates death; obtaining milk requires life. The origin of these foods is in living creatures, and keeping them separate makes us aware of their source.

The Hebrew word for "charity," *tzedakah*, is correctly translated as "justice." We do not look at giving to the poor as something beyond the call of duty; we perceive it as simple justice. Hence we can understand why the Torah prohibits a Jewish farmer from eating the produce of his own field until he has given tithes to those without land of their own. He is not being asked to be extra nice; he is being commanded to be just.

The types of animals we eat are chosen in part for their

symbolism. The ruminants that have split hooves tend to be tranquil, domesticated animals that have no natural weapons. These are animals whose characteristics we may absorb through eating. We may not eat scavengers, carnivores, or birds of prey — these are not characteristics we want to absorb at all.

There is no question that kashrut has contributed to our survival as a distinct nation as well. Jews all over the world have common dietary patterns. I can be confident that the curried hamin of the Calcutta Jews has no milk and meat in its ingredients. When I eat kosher French cuisine I know the meat is not pork and the animals have been slaughtered according to the law. In communities all over the world Jews meet each other at the local kosher bakery, shop at the same stores, and have their own butchers. These laws are a major force in maintaining unity, act as a social barrier against assimilation, and create a feeling of community among the Jewish people.

Another aspect of kashrut is the encouragement of aesthetic sensitivity. Judaism prohibits the consumption of animals that have died of natural causes or that are deformed or diseased; it also prohibits the consumption of insects and loathsome foods. It is possible that one idea behind this is to encourage us to view ourselves with dignity and to act with dignity. One of the best defences against immorality is a strong sense of self-esteem and dignity. Evil should be looked at as beneath our dignity — stealing is stooping too low, gossip is petty and small-minded. In order to help us achieve and maintain this level of dignity the Torah prohibits foods like carcasses and diseased animals.

Some religions seek the path to spirituality through withdrawal from the physical world. A monastic life is glorified; celibacy and asceticism are seen as ideals. Some view the human as essentially an animal that is incapable of elevating itself beyond the struggle for survival; hence they encourage a life of hedonism and materialism. Judaism sees the human as an essentially spiritual being, clothed in a physical body. Judaism maintains that the physical is not evil — it is just not the complete view of reality. Judaism seeks to elevate the physical world, not to deny it nor glorify it. The laws of kashrut allow us to enjoy the pleasures of the physical world, but in such a way that we sanctify and elevate the pleasure through consciousness and sensitivity. Kashrut recognizes that the essential human need is not food, drink, or comfort but meaning. Judaism, through the dietary laws, injects meaning even into something as commonplace and instinctive as eating.

A CHAPLAIN in the Israel Defence Force Reserves, Mordechai Becher has been a senior lecturer at Ohr Somayach Yeshivah in Jerusalem since 1987 and presently also answers questions on the yeshiva's award-winning Web site (www.ohr.org.il) in its "Ask the Rabbi" section. Originally from Australia, he is an internationally renowned speaker and the co-author of *Avutot Ahava: Halachic Issues in Outreach* (Targum Press) and *After the Return: A Guide for the Newly Observant* (Feldheim Publishers), and one of the developers of the Judaica software programs Where in Israel? and Judaica Wizard.

References:

Code of Jewish Law, Orach Chaim 223:6; *Rema* ad loc.

Cohn, Jacob. *The Royal Table.*

Grunfeld, Isidore. *The Jewish Dietary Laws.* London: Soncino Press.

Munk. *Shechita: Religious, Historical and Scientific Perspectives.* New York: Feldheim Publishers, 1976.

Rabbi Yechezkel Landau, *Responsa Noda BiYehudah, Yoreh De'ah* 10.

Simchah, Simchah, Simchah

Holly Pavlov

"**A**re we having fun yet?"

It's a pithy comeback but not a very Jewish sentiment. "Fun" suggests time-bound merriment, joy that has a finite beginning and ending, joy more often than not linked to an activity. This view of happiness is outward-focused, based on things outside the self.

"Fun" is at odds with the Jewish notion of happiness. *Simchah*, Judaism's idea of happiness, has an internal focus; it has nothing to do with having and everything to do with being. *Simchah* is an inner attitude, an acceptance of life's circumstances.

Our Sages teach that there are two kinds of happiness: "*samei'ach b'chelko*" (happiness with one's lot) and "*simchah b'mitzvah*" (happiness in doing God's will). In *The Ethics of Our Fathers* our Sages ask, "Who is rich?" They answer, "One who is happy with his lot."

Inner Peace

Be happy with what you've got. Why? We understand that all one has — one's self, one's talents, one's belongings, and even one's pain — comes directly from God. God gives each person everything she or he needs. God knows who we are, much better than we do, and gives us what we need in life. This may not include everything we want, of course. It may even include suffering.

The people who are happy with their lot in life appreciate all that is given to them even when what seems to be positive is intermingled with what seems to us to be bad. Such a person understands that painful experiences are just as much God's gifts as are the blessings he receives. He views the challenges and trials he faces in his life as opportunities for growth and greater self-awareness.

Happiness with one's lot requires a deep level of self-knowledge. Someone who knows him or herself well is able to set realistic, attainable goals. Not everyone is going to be a world-renowned chemist or a wealthy businessperson; the trick and the challenge is to figure out what special skills God has given you and to determine how you can best use them in the world. To accept your gifts and limitations equally and be content with your lot enables you to use those gifts in a more productive fashion.

By no means does this limit goal-setting or ambition. While it is true that all things come from God, it does not follow that because God has not granted you the fulfillment of a particular goal right now that God intends for you never to reach that goal. For instance, even though you are not married now, it may be God's will that you marry in the future.

You need not set aside the goal, although it does call for an understanding that your life is to be lived on God's timetable, not yours (however displeasing that notion might be at first).

Acceptance of God's will brings with it inner peace

and happiness. This avoids the modern pitfall of pinning satisfaction/ happiness on externalities — career goals, financial success, personal relationships.

In the modern understanding of happiness, it's always something else that will finally make someone happy. This becomes an endless pursuit. Once one goal is achieved, the elusive "happiness" will be attained only through the achievement of something else. Happiness seems always just out of reach. Until the cycle is breached, the poor unhappy soul stays stuck on a merry-go-round of always needing just one more thing.

The Jewish perspective allows one to enjoy each moment as it comes and to appreciate the little things as well as the big. Since the focus is on one's attitude, happiness is never far away.

Harmonic Happiness

There is a second level of happiness: joy in doing what's right.

Every human being is created with a body and soul, two distinct and separate aspects that are often in conflict. What the body wants to do, the soul sometimes says no to and vice versa. The body wants to steal your roommate's pint of ice cream and gobble it down, the soul won't let it. The soul wants to get out of bed and visit a sick person in the hospital, the body wants to roll over and sleep.

The fulfillment of mitzvot, God's commandments, brings into harmony these two dissimilar aspects of being, which in turn fosters a closer connection to God. This is the ultimate happiness. Using one's body to fulfill a mitzvah utilizes one's corporeal being to achieve a purely spiritual goal; this brings both aspects of a person into harmony. Both aspects of the human being are working together as they were meant to.

How does this work? Mitzvot are God's guidebook to productive living, to maximizing each person's potential. They teach how to harness physical activity to heighten spirituality — which way to eat, to dress, to engage in sexual relations. The Torah tells us how to use this world in a way that is beneficial to the body as well as the soul. It is being in this holistic mode that brings an inner harmony and satisfaction to the Jew.

When the body and soul connect, the truest happiness is achieved. And that's a lot more than just having fun.

HOLLY PAVLOV has been teaching and inspiring Jewish women from around the world for three decades. An expert in teaching textual study skills, she is the founder and dean of She'arim College of Jewish Studies for Women in Jerusalem. There she applies her administrative, teaching, and counseling expertise to the Jewish education and spiritual growth of her students.

Connections:
A Jewish Look at Sexuality

Gila Manolson

Human sexuality. It's one of the most powerful forces in our lives. It can leave us sitting among the pieces of broken dreams, or it can help build a lifelong relationship. It can leave us feeling fragmented or whole.

Judaism has a lot of wisdom to offer about expressing our sexuality. It begins, even before relationships, with the issue of self-image. Sexuality and self-definition are inextricably linked. In other words, the way we regard our sexual selves has a lot to do with who we feel ourselves to be.

People have many layers. The most external is our physical selves, our faces and bodies — "what I have." Deeper in lie our talents and abilities — "what I do." And at the very core is our soul — "who I am." If we are not careful, our more external layers may outshine what lies deeper inside, making us appear, both to others and ourselves, to be less than who we truly are.

The Jewish solution is something called *tzniut*. *Tzniut* is usually translated as "modesty," leading many people to believe that (a) it's a dress code, (b) it's only for women, and (c) its purpose is to help religious men (who would be distracted by scantily clad females) keep their minds in the right place. In other words, *tzniut* is a neat way of dumping men's problem on women's doorstep. Yet this is a huge reduction of a profound concept. *Tzniut* is something I cultivate for myself and is relevant whether I'm male or female.

Tzniut begins with the consciousness that my more external layers — starting with my physical self — must not falsely represent me; rather, they should express who I really am. My inner core. My soul.

Too often the way we dress draws attention to our outside rather than to our inside. Societal norms currently don't leave much to the imagination. The message of the more modest dress sanctioned by Jewish sources is: "I am much more than what meets the eye. If you want to see the real me, you'll have to look deeper."

Most people don't want to be appraised primarily for their outside — especially when it comes to relationships. Yet, realizing (as does Judaism) the importance of sexual attraction, they often make the mistake of putting their "external" foot forward first.

A woman named Judy was visiting her friend Laura, who had an important job interview the next morning. Sifting through the clothes in Laura's closet, the two were trying to decide what she should wear.

Judy pulled a miniskirt and tank top from a hanger. "How about this?" she suggested.

Laura looked at her in disbelief. "Are you kidding?" she exclaimed. "I want to be seen as a genuinely serious person, not as a body!"

"Good point, Laura. But when you go out on your first date with a man with whom you're hoping to have a genuinely serious relationship, you don't think twice about wearing such an outfit."

Women, more often than men, fall into the trap of unconsciously defining themselves by their looks (largely because they know how important looks are to men). Men, on the other hand, tend to define themselves by their power and accomplishments. Women fall for being sex objects; men, success objects. Both are selling themselves short. Beauty and achievements should be seen not as our essence, but merely as a part of the much deeper picture that comprises us. Therefore, in Judaism, both genders (and especially women) dress modestly and realize that their greatest achievement is simply becoming a better person.

How we've learned to define ourselves will have profound consequences once we enter the realm of relationships. So, too, will the way we handle sexuality itself.

Jewish tradition affirms sexuality as the most beautiful (and holy) way a husband and wife can express their love for one another. At the same time, you've probably correctly guessed that Judaism doesn't sanction premarital sex. What you may not know is that, traditionally, people don't do premarital anything. They don't even touch.

Here's the idea (or at least one of the ideas) behind it:

Humans are born into the world with a sense of "existential loneliness" — the feeling that beneath all the parties, friends, even family, we're still alone in a very deep way. Consequently, one of the strongest needs we have is to achieve oneness with another person.

Physical contact, starting with touch, plugs right into this need. Touch between two people who are sexually attracted is very subliminally powerful. It brings down the walls between you and your partner, creating feelings of connection and closeness. The problem is that feeling close and being close are two very different things — and can be easily confused. When touch enters a relationship before any real closeness has been achieved, you may be left with a wonderful feeling of closeness which is nothing but illusion.

When touch enters the picture, your objectivity goes down the drain. A magical, rose-colored screen descends before your eyes, filtering out the negative and accentuating the positive in your partner — and often even creating virtues that have no basis in reality. Why? Because now that you feel close, that's what you want to see.

A woman I know was living with her boyfriend for many months before they got married. I visited her shortly after the wedding, and she looked depressed. She told me, "I don't know if my marriage is going to work."

"Oh no," I said in dismay. "What's the matter?"

I'll never forget her unhappy answer. "I don't know if he's deep enough for me."

How could this have happened? As they had been physically involved from quite early in their relationship, the rose-colored screen had always been lowered. But once you get married (for very complex psychological reasons), the screen always lifts. And, painfully, she realized that the depth she had always wanted to see — and that she was certain she did see — simply wasn't there.

Now, if you're dating someone about whom you might someday have to ask yourself, *Is this the person I want to spend the rest of my life with?* and from early on you're doing something which is guaranteed to put blinders on you, you have to admit, this isn't too smart. You wouldn't invest in a car with your vision so severely blurred. Yet because physical contact feels so good and satisfies such a deep need, people let themselves be blinded.

Touch also eclipses the most important form of connection there is. Two people truly become one by first bringing down the walls, not between their bodies, but between their minds and hearts. This requires a lot of intellectual and emotional sharing — in other words, talking. However, you're less likely to invest hours of your relationship in deep conversation, hoping to feel close, when, at the back of your mind, you know there's a foolproof shortcut: getting physical.

Judaism says: Stop. Wait. Before you let the physical side enter, develop a relationship which stands on its own two feet — a true soul-to-soul connection. Once that relationship is truly solid — after marriage — the physical side will be a beautiful and powerful expression of what you have.

There's a big difference between letting sexuality determine an illusory connection and letting it express a real one. Before you give someone the opportunity to appreciate your body, let him or her have the chance to appreciate you for who you truly are. That's the kind of bond that lasts.

These two ideas, *tzniut* and not touching when dating, each convey the same important idea about sexuality, in two different ways. *Tzniut* tells us that we want to define *ourselves* by our inner content. Rather than let our physical selves outshine our spiritual selves, we want to use our outside to send a message about who we are inside. Avoiding touch tells us that we want to define our *relationships* by their inner content. Instead of letting physicality substitute for the real thing, we want to reserve our sexuality until it can express a genuine, spiritual bond.

In both cases, we want our bodies to express our souls. For when they are united in this way, we achieve wholeness.

GILA MANOLSON teaches for the Isralight Institute. She is the author of *The Magic Touch: The Jewish Approach to Relationships* and *Outside/Inside: A Fresh Look at Tzniut*. She lives with her husband and family in the Har Nof neighborhood of Jerusalem.

The Secret Ingredient of a Successful Marriage

Yirmiyohu and Tehilla Abramov

What is the secret, mysterious ingredient necessary for bringing together a couple's disparate personalities? The cementing ingredient is the ultimate in intimacy: physical intimacy.

Physical intimacy is meant to be enjoyable. Thousands of years before Masters and Johnson and the woman's liberation movement, the Jewish tradition recognized the importance of women gaining as much pleasure from physical intimacy as men. One of the obligations of a Jewish husband is to give his wife physical pleasure.

But intimacy is more than just a momentary pleasure. Judaism views physical intimacy as the ultimate vehicle to express emotional intimacy, to create closeness. Therefore Jewish law limited it to a framework where emotional bonding is essential. A person engaging in casual expressions of this most personal aspect of life must become desensitized to the emotional dimension of the experience. This desensitization cripples one emotionally and spiritually. When people thus crippled get married, they have difficulty reawakening their sensitivity and achieving true intimacy.

The complete commitment and emotional closeness of marriage allow physical relations to be the most intense, potent, and powerful experience possible. Such an experience is possible when we conserve and reserve all of our sexuality for our spouse.

People were created in such a way that they are meant to be sensitive to every sight, to the slightest touch. Every interaction between husband and wife is meant to be meaningful, even a hand brushing a shoulder. By directing this intimate side of ourselves to one person only, we preserve and enhance it. Sharing this experience with others, whether through speech, dress, or action, dilutes its power. It's a sad truth that we are the most overexposed generation in history.

Since physical relations play a significant role in the cementing of a marriage, it is of paramount importance that they are always meaningful and enjoyable. One of the most commonly encountered problems in marriage is boredom with physical intimacy, which inevitably creates tension and can contribute to the souring of a relationship. Dr. Domeena Renshaw, head of the Sexual Dysfunction Clinic of Chicago's Loyola University, states that 80 percent of the divorces in Western society come about because of dysfunction within the couple's intimate lives. Furthermore, 50 percent of the couples who remain married have problems in this area. Familiarity breeding contempt is certainly a significant factor in these problems.

The most natural solution to such a situation, in order to invigorate the relationship, is a temporary cessation of physical contact. (This does not mean emotional distance.) Researchers experimented with this concept and found that it worked beautifully — in the lab. As soon as the couple went home, though, their self-imposed separation agreement didn't work. They began to find exceptions to the rules they'd created, which brought about confusion, tension, and misunderstanding.

Jewish tradition avoids such ambivalence and ambiguity by employing an objective physiological factor — menstruation — to determine the times of physical closeness and separation. This divinely ordained system, called "taharat hamishpachah" (family purity), mandates a complete cessation of physical contact between husband and wife during the time of the woman's menstrual cycle (a minimum of five days) and for seven days following the cessation of bleeding. The woman checks to ascertain when her period has ended and continues to check that there is no bleeding during the subsequent seven days.

The guesswork is removed; the subtle pressures are eliminated. The onset of the menses signifies a change in status in the relationship, during which time husband and wife are not permitted to have physical relations with one another: they don't sleep in the same bed together, nor do they touch each other. Because it is total, the separation enhances physical intimacy when they join together. The goal of this system is to increase awareness and appreciation of physical expressions, making every touch count. Even a good-night kiss should not be a perfunctory ritual, but an expression of love and desire.

Too often, a couple uses physical expression to hide the lack of emotional connection underneath. The physical distance mandated by taharat hamishpachah enables the couple to focus on other methods of interaction. The distance gives them space to communicate on a different level and to be friends with each other. This emphasis on communication then carries over into the time when there is no separation, creating emotional intimacy. Couples who follow this Jewish law find it the glue that holds their relationship together, even when they observe no other Jewish law.

The period of separation also gives us an opportunity for individuality, a period of privacy within the total togetherness of marriage. And it reflects respect for the woman's biological well-being. A woman's vaginal discharges are slightly acidic and serve as a natural barrier to infection. During her period, this discharge shifts to alkaline, and the natural barrier is lost. It takes about a week for the normal acidity to be restored. The uterine channel is also in a vulnerable state, having shed the protective uterine lining, and it takes seven days from the end of menstruation for this lining to re-form. Thus, research has shown that a woman is more susceptible to infection during her period and for the seven days following.

Dr. Alexander Gunn, a renowned British researcher, published the following: "Jewish principles which require couples to abstain from intercourse for a certain number of days after the end of menstruation may be playing their part in protecting the woman. The cells on the surface of the cervix are known to be most susceptible to damage just after menstruation." This explains another study which has shown that women who observe *taharat hamishpachah* are twenty times less likely to suffer from cervical cancer than women who do not observe these laws.

But the separation, ultimately, is a means to an end. It is intended to build emotional closeness between husband and wife so that when they do come together physically they can express this closeness to the utmost. Marital relations are a physical culmination of a relationship which in its totality should be loving, caring, and emotionally fulfilling.

At the end of seven spotless days the woman bathes thoroughly so she can immerse in a mikveh, a collection of natural waters. This immersion is not intended to cleanse. Rather, the woman passing through these waters once again changes her status and joins her husband intimately.

The symbolism of the mikveh is multifaceted. The mikveh waters are called *mayim chayim*, "living waters." Water sustains all life; from the rain on the crops to the water in our cells, we are all nourished by water. Thus, at the moment when a couple can renew physical relations, the woman passes through the mikveh as a kind of rebirth. And because the mikveh also symbolizes the rivers of Eden, it serves as a reconnection with the ultimate Source of life and with the spiritual perfection symbolized by the Garden of Eden.

When the woman returns home from the mikveh, she and her husband rejoice in each other and their renewed physical contact. In fact, having marital relations is termed "the commandment of joy." After the separation, this reunion is intended to be a loving, passionate expression of the couple's feelings. It is the wedding night all over again, a rediscovery of each other. With such a cycle of physical separation and reunion, bound together with the thread of emotional connection, a Jewish couple has the key to the golden chain that has enabled the Jewish people to survive through the centuries.

Tourists to Massada, the mountaintop desert fortress in Israel where a group of Jews made a last-ditch effort some two thousand years ago to resist the Romans, are often amazed upon seeing the several ancient *mikva'ot* that were built by these desperate and beleaguered Jews who, despite their dire circumstances, observed *taharat hamishpachah*. But it should come as no surprise — the observance of *taharat hamishpachah* is central to being Jewish. The act of faith embodied in the wife using the mikveh in order to rejoin physically with her husband is the most powerful ritual in Judaism, because it is the factor that has bound the Jewish family together through millennia. And the Jewish family is the heart and soul of the Jewish people.

YIRMIYOHU AND TEHILLA ABRAMOV are well-known educators who specialize in the field of marriage and family life. They are the authors of *Our Family, Our Strength: Creating a Jewish Home*, *Two Halves of a Whole: Torah Guidelines for Marriage*, *Harmony in the Home: An Educational Program for the Jewish Family*, *The Secret of Jewish Femininity: Insights into the Practice of Taharat HaMispacha*, and *Straight from the Heart: A Torah Perspective on Mothering Through Nursing* (all published by Targum Press). They are also the founders of Jewish Marriage Education (JME: POB 43206, Jerusalem 91431), a nonprofit international organization dedicated to bringing a deeper understanding of marriage and family life to the Jewish community.

What Is Your Potential?

Denah Weinberg

Dreams have meaning.
I once had a dream.

My dream was that one day all the animals in the zoo woke up and did not know who they were. The monkey didn't know it was a monkey, the giraffe didn't know it was a giraffe, and the hippopotamus didn't know it was a hippopotamus. They didn't know what sounds to make, they didn't know what food to eat, and they didn't know when or how to sleep. It was bedlam.

Then I awoke and realized something. This is also true about people. *We don't know who or what we are.* And if we don't know who we are, *then we don't know what our potential is.*

I can't know my potential before I know who I am. I can't know where to go, what to accomplish, or what dreams I can realize. And if I don't reach my potential, can I be happy? Can an artist feel fulfilled if he isn't painting? Can a musician feel fulfilled if he isn't performing?

What, exactly, is human potential?

Pirkei Avot (Ethics of the Fathers) teaches that mankind is beloved by God because He created each of us with a soul.

Our soul contains the secret to unlocking our human potential. People are not just four-legged animals standing on two feet. We are different from animals: we have free will. We can choose, animals cannot.

Animals work on instinct, which they cannot disobey. A lion, for example, cannot "will" itself to lie peacefully next to a sheep. A dog cannot "will" itself to become a vegetarian.

Humans, however, can choose to act contrary to their nature. A lazy person can motivate himself to be more industrious. An impulsive person can train himself to think before he acts. Because we have a soul, which is defined as "free will," we have the power to create our own destiny.

It's great to know we can be more than we are, and, if only we try, we can be whatever we want to be! Free will is the language of our soul.

Pirkei Avot adds that God expresses even greater love for us by telling us about this soul, for then we can tap into its potential.

Let us imagine a beggar, destitute and starving, begging on the street for his bread. One day, he gets a letter from a lawyer stating that his long-lost uncle died and left him a million dollars. This letter is in the mailbox — but the beggar doesn't know about it yet. The question is, Is this beggar rich or poor?

I believe the answer is that the beggar is poor, but he is potentially rich. Unless and until he is made aware of his treasure, however, that potential will not be realized.

When we realize we have a God-given soul, and understand its capacity for greatness, it becomes much more valuable and useful to us, just as when the beggar finds out he has the million dollars it will be useful to him and help him improve his life.

Did you ever observe parents of a newborn baby? They have a passionate need to identify this child as looking like them, their parents, or their siblings. Friends and other family members also join in this passion. "This baby looks like his grandfather on his mother's side," exclaims an uncle. "No," insists an aunt, "he looks just like Uncle Joey on his father's side. . . ."

Why do they care who this child resembles? It's a new creature; maybe it resembles no one.

This phenomenon, this need to identify the newborn child, happened at the birth of the parents of this baby and at the births of their parents and their grandparents. It happens with each person all the way back through the generations to Cain and Abel.

And who did Cain and Abel look like? Their father and mother, Adam and Eve, of course!

And who did Adam and Eve look like?

Their "Father," God.

They were created, as the Torah states, "in the image of God."

What, indeed, is this "image"? God has no body, no hands, no feet, no eyes, no ears. So how do men and women — all mankind — resemble God?

Before I answer, I want to ask you, Do you think Picasso fulfilled his potential? Mozart? Albert Einstein? Sigmund Freud? General MacArthur? Princess Diana?

Those who claim these personalities "fulfilled their potential" are really talking about their talents. Indeed, these personalities excelled in their talents, but talents belong to the individual. Potential is the possession of all humanity.

Mankind resembles God in that we all possess the same universal potential: all of us, all of humanity, are made in the image of God. It has no boundaries. It represents excellence to the highest degree. And it always expresses itself in the most goodness, righteousness, morality, and virtue that can be achieved.

A bond exists between all of humanity. When a person involves himself in developing a talent, he becomes special in that specific area and separates himself from most other people. But when a person develops his spiritual potential, he can more readily unite with others.

I know some great doctors who are not such great people, or great parents or great spouses or great friends. And sometimes they're not even happy with their own achievements. I know some great financial leaders who are workaholics and neglect their spouses, children, community, and selves.

In Judaism, realizing one's potential means being a man or woman who excels in all areas, spiritual as well as social. He is a good spouse, a good parent, a good friend, and one who is good to himself. She is well balanced, using her talents to accomplish in the physical world while excelling as a "human being" (in the spiritual sense). He possesses a noble character, has developed a love for everyone, is responsible in all areas, and, last but not least, excels in being a happy person.

In Judaism, reaching your potential means becoming a total person, a special human being. By consciously using our free will to maximize our potential, we too can fulfill the goal of Creation. We can all be Godlike.

Once there was a man who was kidnapped, put on a plane, and sent across the ocean. When the plane landed, the kidnappers took the man out, released the ropes that bound him, opened the blindfold, and set him free.

What did he do?

He started asking questions: Where am I? Why am I here? What should I do here? What do I eat here? What do I wear here? What language do they speak here?

As adults we are in the same position. When we were children, we couldn't understand what was the purpose of life. Now, tens of years later, we need to "wake up" and ask ourselves: Where am I? Who put me here? Why am I here? What should I accomplish here? *What is my potential?*

By the way, our Torah tells us happiness is the key that unlocks potential. Any happiness — whether in friendship, in experiencing nature's beauty, in enjoying good food, in acquiring anything from new clothes to a tennis racquet to the latest-model Porsche — gives us power and drive to pursue our potential to the fullest.

All happiness opens the heart. If we are happy with the little things, this creates a backdrop for advancing toward a human being's greatest achievement: actualizing his potential. In fact, nothing can be actualized — no talent, career, or accomplishment — without a happy attitude. We can reach our potential only when we are happy.

In order to plant a field, a farmer first plows the earth to prepare it. Then he can plant the seeds and they will grow. Happiness is the plowing. Potential is the seeds. Be happy and dream of how you can reach your potential.

Living Judaism brings happiness — happiness in daily life and happiness through meaning in life. Judaism opens this path to maximizing human potential.

Our spiritual potential is waiting (impatiently!) to be actualized. It pushes us and says, "Please be aware of me. Please pay attention to me. I'm your potential, and I need to be actualized." It adds, "I can never be happy if I'm not actualized, and you can't be happy, either." It makes us a promise: "Make me happy and I'll make you happy."

It's not hard. The instructions are in the Book. Small steps lead to bigger steps and bigger gains on the road to becoming a "total person." Judaism is the way to self-actualization, to self-awareness, to constant, continuous, and sure happiness.

Reaching our potential is the ultimate success in life. It is available. It's the key to a happy life. It's in the Book and the Book is yours.

DENAH WEINBERG is dean and director of Aish HaTorah College for Women in Jerusalem (E.Y.A.H.T.). Born and educated in Far Rockaway, N.Y., she has lived in Israel for many years. She has been a world-renowned lecturer for over three decades and has helped thousands of women to grow and maximize their potential to greatness.

How Much Good Is "Good Enough"?

Lynn Finson

Imagine a bedraggled bag lady clothed in rags. She could be from any major urban area. Her heavy legs can barely carry her; open sores mark her half-bare feet. Her hair is matted and looks like it has not been washed for at least several months. She smells so bad you almost gag when she gets near. She is pushing a cart full of old newspapers and a cardboard box she probably sleeps in at night. As she closes in on you, you have a few choices:

1. You can put on your best New York glazed "I don't see you" look and walk by.

2. Perhaps being skeptical as to what she will do with your money, you give her a token amount and move on.

3. You immediately dip into your pocket and give her all the coins or bills you have. You might even offer her some food if you are lucky enough to have a spare sandwich on you.

Many times we think being "good enough" means enacting kindness at a level that is comfortable for us financially and emotionally. How does the honest person, the person who considers him or herself an ethical person, ever know that his or her response was "good enough"? If you responded to the bag lady with some of above choices, you have done something good. But was it enough? Was your choice based on pity, disgust, or inner kindness?

In a similar vein, our rabbis have discussed the differences between Abraham and Job, noting that while Job would serve his guests what they were accustomed to, Abraham would actually educate his guests by introducing them to many of the finer things in life; for example, even if they could never afford a steak dinner and would have been happy with bread and radishes, Abraham gave them the experience of eating a steak dinner. Surely Abraham would not have given the bag lady a few coins; he would have built her a shelter which would provide for her physical, emotional, and spiritual needs. His level of kindness was of a highly developed nature. To Abraham finding opportunities to do acts of kindness was a lifelong quest. Abraham's kindness possessed an urgency to it begging to be expressed in dozens of ways.

There is an oral tradition concerning Noah's ark that may help us understand giving in a new light. It tells us that the year Noah and his family spent in the ark no one ever got a good night's rest. The animals had different feeding schedules, and Noah was required to meet those demands. Once he delayed feeding the lion and it bit him. He suffered dearly for his tardiness.

Let us put this in context. The man had just spent a great deal of time building a boat that his whole society mocked him for. He also must have had a terrible time dealing with the loss of the world as he knew it, and to top it off a lion goes and bites him. One might ask here, Couldn't God have made it a little easier for Noah?

To answer this question, we must first know why the world was destroyed by the flood in the first place. The great medieval commentator Rashi states that a primary reason the world was destroyed by the flood was because it had developed into a society of takers, a society built on theft. This is the antithesis of what God had intended when He created the world. This world was meant to be one of giving. The pre-flood world had simply lost its raison d'être. There is a verse in Psalms that states, "Olam chesed yibaneh — The world will be built on the blueprint of kindness." The pre-flood world had strayed too far, and it was too late for them.

God wanted to give humanity a second chance, so He told Noah to build the boat. He arranged a situation that would indelibly imprint in the very spiritual makeup of all those on the ark the concept of constant unconditional giving — the constant need of the animals for care and attention. The ark contained the entirety of the human race, and as such was a microcosm of the future world, a world that would demand that people help each other in order to survive and grow physically as well as spiritually. What better way to imprint this in the world than to train the future inhabitants in the womb of the ark? He therefore had the ark's inhabitants constantly giving in order that the concept become part of them.

The act of creating a world is an act of birth, a gift of tremendous worth. God wanted us to partake of His world in all its beauty and glory. As a matter of fact, our Sages tell us that at the end of a person's life one of the things a person will be asked by the Heavenly court is "Did you enjoy My world?" Imagine, God Himself wants to know if we took the time to smell the flowers, to see the sun rise and set, to enjoy the wonder each day brings. In each aspect of God's creation we can see the infinite giving involved whether we speak of the miracle of day turning into night or water flowing or the sun warming us. As the children of God, created in His image, we are meant to learn to be givers, emulating His ways.

As God's goodness has no end, so our giving can grow and improve endlessly. One of the distinguishing features of Jewish ethics is that one can never rest on his laurels. Most of us are not able to build shelters for every homeless person we meet, like Abraham would have done. But we must strive to be the type of person that would build them, understanding that God Himself is the Source of giving.

LYNN FINSON currently serves as Educational Director of Midreshet Rachel College of Jewish Studies for Women, a division of Darche Noam Institutions. Midreshet Rachel has long been dedicated to providing a sophisticated program of Torah study to motivated students. Prior to her current position, the author was a counselor at Bruriah High School and a teacher and counselor at Yeshiva University High School. She taught a broad range of classes at the Jewish Heritage Center of Queens and at seminaries in Israel.

Men and Women:
The Jewish View

Tzippora Heller

To get a clear picture of the Jewish view of womanhood, we must go back to the beginning: the Torah.

In the beginning of Genesis, the Torah chooses to refer to Adam in the plural tense: "God created the man in His image; in the image of God He created him, male and female He created them. And God blessed them" (Genesis 1:27–28). Why "them"? This was before the creation of Eve!

The oral tradition provides us with a fascinating insight into this grammatical oddity. The first human, it tells us, was really an androgynous being, both male and female in one body: a sophisticated, self-sufficient human being.

But if God had created such a complete human being, why the later separation into two parts, into Adam and Eve? The answer given in the Jewish tradition is that God did not want this first human creation to be alone, for it would then possess an illusion of self-sufficiency. Note that there is no word for "independence" in classical Hebrew (what we use now, atzma'ut, is a modern creation). The concept of independence doesn't exist in Jewish tradition. Aside from God, nothing and no one is really independent. Since we are supposed to ingrain into ourselves that God is the source of every-thing, self-sufficiency would have been a spiritual defeat.

God wanted to fashion the human being into two sepa-rate people in order to create a healthy situation of depend-ence, yearning, and mutual giving. Human beings are not meant to be alone because then they would have no one to give to, no one to grow with, and nothing to strive for. To ac-tualize oneself spiritually, a human being cannot be alone.

But why, then, didn't God create two identical beings? The answer is that in order to maximize giving, the recipient must be different from the giver. If the two are identical, giving can occur, but it is limited. One would give based on his or her own needs, since the receiver would have the exact same needs. To truly be a giver, the person must take into account what the re-ceiver needs and not only what the giver wants. By giving to someone with different needs, a person is trained to think and give on terms other than his or her own.

We see, then, that the separation had to be into two different beings, in order for us to learn to appreciate, love, give, and care for those unlike ourselves. This is fundamental to all moral and spiritual growth. We can also understand why God didn't just create two beings from the start: by starting as one, we can know and feel that our life partners are our true complement, that we need them and the differ-ences just as they need us and ours.

What Are the Differences?

The Torah is a path to self-actualization, to spiritual growth. We have seen that in order to grow, a person cannot be alone. Therefore two beings were created. To maximize growth, the beings need to be different, and so men and women were created as different beings. But what are these differences?

In the Creation story, the way in which God separates man and woman provides us with an insightful look at gender differences. We will briefly discuss here some of the most powerful differences. Note the feminine-masculine polarities we will discuss do not apply exactly the same way to each man and woman — we were all created as unique individuals. However, what the Torah describes does exist for everyone to some degree.

Internality

Interestingly enough, Adam was not split down the middle; rather, Eve was created from an internal organ: his rib. By mentioning the rib, the Torah is teaching us a principle in understanding the nature of masculine and feminine strengths: feminine manifestation and strength is more internal, while the masculine focus and expression is more external. The way the feminine internality is most observed is through the enormous weight women place on relationships, which by definition are personal and private. Several thousand years later, popular psychology confirms this key distinction: Dr. John Gray has as a major theme of his bestselling book (*Men Are from Mars, Women Are from Venus* [New York: Thorsons, 1992]) the idea that women are more what he calls "relationship-based" than men.

This emphasis on the internal has many practical implications. While most of Judaism applies equally to men and women, including the central ideas of celebrating Shabbat and keeping kosher, not all commandments apply in the same way. The Torah's system of spiritual achievement and happiness will apply differently to the two genders. For example, women who are more internal and in a sense private will usually find their direct connection to God most efficiently through private prayer, and therefore Judaism encourages them to express this through regular daily private prayer, although of course they can pray in a synagogue if they prefer. Men are more external (we see evidence of this in the world at large also, in that men are more drawn to be part of a group or team). This is part of the masculine spiritual makeup and explains why man's spiritual path is more related to public prayer — it helps men grow.

Binah

The Torah also describes the process of Eve's creation using the word *vayiven*, "God built." The Hebrew word for "understanding" or "insight" is *binah*, which shares the same root. This suggests, as it says in the Talmud, that women have *binah yeteirah*, an extra dose of wisdom and understanding. This is much greater than "women's intuition": it means entering something and understanding it from the inside, what has been called "inner reasoning." Men tend to have more of what is called *da'at*, understanding something from the outside, often more connected to facts and figures. Society loses an enormous asset when only one of these intellectual aspects is valued. Just as two eyes make our view of things more accurate, seeing things from the two different male and female perspectives makes our understanding of life more complete.

Note that modern science supports Judaism's age-old contention that men and women's minds work differently. Research by Ralph Holloway and Christine de Lacoste-Utamsing, Jeanette McGlone, and Doreen Kimura (see the fourth section of M. Kaufman's *Feminism and Judaism* [Jerusalem: Heritage Press, 1996] for a comprehensive summary) has proven beyond a doubt that men and women's brains are physically quite different. Social scientists more and more look to physiology as the source of different behaviors and ways of thinking, as well as a determining factor in areas of interest and excellence.

Conclusion

Gender is a pivotal quality in each person's identity. Men and women are fully equal but different — and that difference is good. With their own unique talents and natures they can give to one another and help each other along the road of life. So God, in His infinite wisdom, created humans as two distinct genders in order to enable them to complement and fulfill each other. Each gender should appreciate and use its special strengths. Seeing as the genders are different, it would be counterproductive to force them to conduct themselves identically: what helps a man won't necessarily help a woman and vice versa.

King Solomon's beautiful poem "*Eishes Chayil*" (A woman of valor) describes all the different roles a woman can have, including teacher, businesswoman, mother, wife — but all of them as a woman. When a person is asked what she does, she often responds with her career. But the truth is that we are not merely doctors, engineers, secretaries, educators. We are human beings trying to fulfill our unique potential. By giving her the tools to grow morally and spiritually while maximizing her unique strengths, the Torah frees a woman to be herself with self-esteem and joy — and no apologies.

TZIPPORA HELLER is an internationally known lecturer and scholar of Jewish studies. Since 1980 she has been a full-time faculty member of Neve Yerushalayim College in Jerusalem, where her areas of expertise include textual analysis of Biblical literature.

Jewish philosophy, and the role of women in Judaism, as well as analyses of the lives of women in the books of the Bible and Prophets. She has been a visiting lecturer at Hebrew University, the Weizman Institute, the University of Haifa, and many other institutions in and out of Israel and is the author of *More Precious than Pearls: Qualities of the Ideal Woman* (Feldheim Publishers) and the soon-to-be published *Our Bodies, Our Souls.*

Editors Note: For more on women and Judaism, see the soon-to-be published Jewish Matters for Women, a collection of essays by Jewish women for Jewish women.

Ask Me a Question

Rabbi Avraham Edelstein

When people discover I'm an observant Jew, their curiosity is often piqued. There are many philosophical questions that are asked, but often, as I meet people in more informal circumstances, the questions are of a more practical nature. I thought I'd briefly share a few common questions and answers:

Q: Don't all of Judaism's rules stifle your individuality?

A: The huge majority of hours of a person's day are completely "individualistic." I spend them very differently from my neighbor, who is also observant. Whom I marry, what I do for a living, where I live, who my friends are, what my family life is like — all these have no fixed regulations. Each individual does exactly as he or she pleases.

Despite this, there are many common things that everybody does, which, at first glance, could seem to stifle individuality — same prayers, same Shabbat, same kosher food laws. Do I feel that these squash the individual "me"?

Let me explain in the following way. Beethoven's 9th Symphony is an exquisite creation. The tapestry of sounds is some of the most powerful music ever created by a human being. The score that all orchestras use when playing is exactly the same. Yet if you go to more than one recital, you may be surprised: the same piece of music can sound completely different when performed by different orchestras. Two recitals by two different orchestras, or even by the same orchestra on different nights, may both be wonderful and beautiful but completely different experiences.

True individuality lies in taking a beautiful piece of music, with fixed notes, and making it come alive in your own unique way. God gave us a beautiful piece of music to play, and it is called the Torah, but how to play it really depends on the individual.

Q: Wouldn't I be a hypocrite if I did only some mitzvot?

A: Judaism regards any mitzvah a person does to be of value. It is not an all-or-nothing process. Let's say an observant person was eating a sandwich when he remembered halfway through that he forgot to say a blessing. Should he go on eating the sandwich without the blessing? Would it be hypocritical to say a blessing after enjoying eating half of it?

Let's up the stakes. Let's say he purposefully decided not to say the blessing, and then he changed his mind halfway through eating the sandwich and then made the blessing. Would his blessing be taken seriously? The answer is yes! Every individual act a person does makes a difference.

The great Chassidic master the Kotzker Rebbe once said that if you think you are finished, you are finished. His point was that we all have much improvement left to do. The key is to realize that there are still steps to be taken. And it doesn't matter if you never observed a mitzvah in your life or if you are the greatest living sage on the face of the earth. If you are still living on this earth, then you still have a reason to be here — you have room yet to grow. So if you haven't reached perfection, join the club. Where you are is important, but what really counts is not where you are. What counts is where you want to be and what effort you put into getting there.

Q: I like being part of the world. Doesn't Judaism take you out of it?

A: Have you ever heard of a Jewish monastery or convent? They never existed and they can't, because Judaism focuses on getting as much out of the world as possible. It doesn't take you out of the world — it enriches your experience in the world. There is nothing more delicious than Shabbat dinner. You are supposed to get married and have a loving, fulfilling relationship with your spouse. Go into your local Jewish bookstore to experience the richness and variety of Jewish music. Judaism does not advocate denying the world and its pleasures; it advocates using them, sanctifying them, channeling them in positive ways. We should all lead full, rich lives.

Of course we admire the holy sage most of all, but observant Jews have included prime ministers, United States senators, Nobel prize–winning writers, supreme court judges, educators, architects, journalists, world-class scientists, poets, and artists. In Jerusalem one of the head veterinarians at the zoo is an observant woman.

Throughout history outstanding leaders in all fields of endeavor have come from the great sages of Judaism. Maimonides was considered the foremost philosopher of his time, and his medical textbooks were studied throughout the world. The prophetess Deborah was our leading soldier and stateswoman.

Do I think Judaism takes you out of the world? To the contrary. The more I learn to incorporate Judaism into my everyday activities, the more I realize how much meaning, purpose, understanding, and, yes, joy Judaism adds to my life.

I hope these questions and answers have been of interest to you.

Please stop by for a visit next time you are in Jerusalem!

AVRAHAM EDELSTEIN is executive director of the Heritage House, which includes free Jewish hostels for men and women in the Old City of Jerusalem.

A Jewish Approach to Death

Leah Kohn

For four years, it was my privilege to work with Rabbi Yitzchak Kirzner, my codirector at the Jewish Renaissance Center in Manhattan. He was brilliant and kind and funny — all the things that make us cherish a person. He was a mentor to literally thousands — students, coworkers, and many others with whom he came into contact. The death of someone close — especially if that person is very young — is a bewildering experience. How are we to understand such an event? How are we to cope with our anguish for the young family Rabbi Kirzner left behind? How are we to deal with our pain?

I won't attempt to deal here with the issue of why good people suffer, a classic topic that deserves its own dedicated study. Rather, I would like to discuss the Jewish approach to death — the way our tradition teaches us to view and cope with personal tragedies of this proportion.

I learned that Rabbi Kirzner had a melanoma, cancer of the most deadly variety, several years ago. Virtually no one else knew. My husband and I had to know, because we were working with Rabbi Kirzner and he would be away for treatments and would be unable to teach for weeks at a time. Rabbi Kirzner asked us not to discuss his condition with anyone.

The news of his illness shocked me. I came home that day dumbfounded. I said to my husband, "How? How could God want to take away a person so important to so many? I'm not even asking how God could allow such a wonderful person to suffer, but from my own selfish viewpoint, how could such a person be taken away?"

A person can spend a lifetime studying the wisdom in just one book of Jewish knowledge. Yet, in this world at least, there are areas beyond our vision, concepts and events we can't figure out. Sometimes it's our very inability that makes us realize God's greatness. Certainly, Rabbi Kirzner privately struggled to figure out what God was doing to him. I was not privy to those struggles, but one thing was evident: rather than weakening him, they gave him awesome strength and, at the same time, a tremendous trust in God.

A year later, Rabbi Kirzner was scheduled to deliver an evening lecture. That day he had received biopsy results which were not good. The topic of Rabbi Kirzner's lecture that night was prayer. He spoke about prayers that are answered and prayers that are not answered. His delivery was so cogent, so smooth, that no one in the audience would have guessed his terrible secret. He said that in truly hard times when we try everything humanly possible to help ourselves, yet still feel events are beyond our control, we must not just pray to God, but throw ourselves on Him. We should tell God: "I'm yours. I know You love me, and I can trust You implicitly. You are doing whatever is best for me, and I'm throwing myself on You."

Rabbi Kirzner's strength was apparent in his calm that evening, as well as on a day-to-day basis. For three years he underwent agonizing chemotherapy, yet none of his students or colleagues suspected he was ill. Although he missed teaching for weeks at a time, he always returned to class with the same delicious wit, the same calm disposition, the same hopefulness in what life has to offer.

On the Friday morning he died, I myself was shocked by the news, even though I knew all along that only a miracle would save him. Toward the end, things were so bad it should have been plain to me what was coming. Yet his dedication to life and his refusal to succumb to depression had swept me along.

I struggled through my own feelings of injustice when I heard the news. Rabbi Kirzner had helped so many. How could this be fair? The answer is, it's not fair — if your measuring stick is life in this world only. Reality for all of us is our everyday lives. Intellectually, we know there is life after life, but this awareness does not participate in our daily reality. In truth, life here is only a preparation for life after life.

How is it a preparation? The kind of life we live here creates the afterlife we will receive after death. We are not passive players — we actively shape our eternity through thoughts, deeds, and our desire to connect with the eternal. Certainly, for Rabbi Kirzner, who created moment to moment goodness, the afterlife is a place of spiritual pleasure unimaginable to us.

We might wonder whether he could have earned a better eternity if only he'd had more time here. Not so. Our earnings in the World to Come are based solely on the degree to which we actualize our potential. Quality rather than quantity of deeds is the measure. All factors are taken into account, including how we overcome life's difficulties.

Each Jew is uniquely precious to God. We have different talents and circumstances, because we each have a different mission in life, a unique aspect of Godliness to contribute. In many cases, a short life span indicates a mission accomplished.

There's a famous story about the Chazon Ish, a pious man and great Torah scholar, who lived in Israel about thirty-five years ago. Bedridden at the end of his life, he studied and even taught from his bed. One day, when a married couple and their child, who had Down's syndrome, came for a blessing, the Chazon Ish stood up as they entered. After the family left, his startled students asked whether he had stood up to honor the parents for their exhaustiing efforts with the child. The Chazon Ish said no — he had stood to honor the child.

The Chazon Ish's reply was an eye-opener. Jewish tradition teaches us that almost all of us alive today have been here before in a different incarnation. We return to this world in order to complete our missions. Each time we return, we're given what we need — intellect, communal support, health, money — to finish our task. If a person, such as a disabled child, is born with limited resources, it means he has little to accomplish. In his previous life, he all but accomplished what his soul had set out to do in the first place. "That is why I stood," said the Chazon Ish.

So from the point of view of the person who has finished his mission, death is neither negative nor a punishment. Our Sages describe death as "a night between two days," a passage from one stage of life to another, from finite to infinite.

But what about those of us left here? How do we deal with our grief? It's not easy, but our task is to trust that God will never leave us alone. Individuals leave, but God is always here for us, and He blesses us with the ability to form new attachments in this world. There are no substitutes for those we have loved and lost, but there are new routes for our love to follow. While adjusting to loss is difficult, we know that God continues to provide for our needs.

We must learn from death the meaning and purpose of life. What should we dedicate ourselves to? The night before Rabbi Kirzner entered the hospital for the last time, he made an appointment to meet with a stranger who had heard a few lectures on tape and felt a half-hour with the rabbi would do him good. Rabbi Kirzner did not mention his illness. Where did he find the will to deal with a stranger's problems at a time when he could have been justifiably preoccupied? Herein lies the remarkable message of Judaism: "I am alive! Thank God, I have time to accomplish something!" In his final moments, Rabbi Kirzner continued to live in his matchless way.

God loves us to a degree no human can match or comprehend. In this supreme love, He often presents us with opportunities for growth that from our perspective seem painful. We can only struggle to accept the ultimate good beyond our limited understanding of God's plan.

The Chiddushei HaRim, a renowned nineteenth-century chassidic rabbi, lived through a tremendous personal tragedy. His daughter died just days after the birth of her ninth child. On hearing of her death, the rabbi said, "Only the Master of mercy can cause such pain." Master of mercy. This is the essence of the Jewish approach to suffering. We trust that an act of God's love is sometimes painful and hard to comprehend. This faith empowers us to move on in life and to learn profound lessons from life's most difficult moments.

LEAH KOHN is the cofounder and director of the Jewish Renaissance Center, a unique learning institution in Manhattan exclusively for Jewish women with little or no background who wish to learn about Judaism. A twelfth-generation Jerusalemite, she has over thirty years of experience in teaching and directing schools in Israel and the United States.

Our God

The Big Bang
and the Big Question:
A Universe without God?*

Lawrence Kelemen

Until the early twentieth century, astronomers entertained three possible models of the universe:

1. The universe could be static. According to this theory, though the mutual gravitational attractions of stars and planets might hold them together in the form of solar systems and galaxies, each of these stellar-terrestrial groups slide through space along its own random trajectory, unrelated to the courses tracked by other groups of stars and planets. The static model works for atheists and believers: Such a universe could have been created by God at some point in history, but it also could have existed forever without God.

2. The universe could be oscillating. It might be a cosmic balloon alternately expanding and contracting. For a few

---

* This essay presents an extremely abbreviated version of the cosmological argument. For a more detailed presentation see the author's essay in *Permission to Believe* (Jerusalem: Targum/Feldheim, 1990).

billion years it would inflate, expanding into absolute nothingness. But the gravitational attraction of every star and planet pulling on every other would eventually slow this expansion until the whole process would reverse and the balloon would come crashing back in upon itself. All that existed would eventually smash together at the universe's center, releasing huge amounts of heat and light, spewing everything back out in all directions and beginning the expansion phase all over again. Such a universe could also have been created by God or could have existed forever without God.

3. Finally, the universe could be open. It might be a cosmic balloon that never implodes. If the total gravitational attraction of all stars and planets could not halt the initial expansion, as in the oscillating model, the universe would spill out into nothingness forever. Eventually the stars would burn out and a curtain of frozen darkness would enshroud all existence. Such a universe could never bring itself back to life. It would come into existence at a moment in history, blaze gloriously, and then pass into irrevocable night.

Crucially, the latter model proposes that before the one-time explosion, all the universe's matter and energy was contained in a singularity, a tiny dot that sat stable in space for eternity before it detonated. This model proposes a paradox: Objects at rest — like the initial singularity — remain at rest unless acted upon by an outside force; and yet, since the initial dot contained all matter and energy, nothing (at least, nothing natural) existed outside of this singularity that could have caused it to explode. The simplest resolution of the paradox is to posit that something supernatural kicked the universe into being. The open model of the universe thus implies a supernatural Creator — a God.

In 1916 Albert Einstein released the first drafts of his general theory of relativity, and the scientific world went wild. It appeared that Einstein had revealed the deepest secrets of the universe. His equations also caused a few problems — technical dilemmas, mathematical snags — but not the sort of thing to interest newspapers or even popular science journals.

Two scientists noticed the glitches. Late in 1917 the Danish astronomer Willem de Sitter reviewed general relativity and returned a detailed response to Einstein, outlining the problem and proposing a radical solution: general relativity could work only if the entire universe was exploding, erupting out in all directions from a central point. Einstein never responded to de Sitter's critique. Then, in 1922, Soviet mathematician Alexander Friedmann independently derived de Sitter's solution. If Einstein was right, Friedmann predicted, the universe must be expanding in all directions at high speed.

Meanwhile, across the sea, American astronomer Vesto Slipher actually witnessed the universe's explosive outward movement. Using the powerful telescope at Lowell Observatory in Flagstaff, Arizona, Slipher discovered that dozens of galaxies were indeed rocketing away from a central point.

Between 1918 and 1922, de Sitter, Friedmann, and Slipher independently shared their findings with Einstein, but he strangely resisted their solution — as if, in his brilliance, he realized the theological implications of an exploding universe. Einstein even wrote a letter to *Zeitschrift fur Physik*, a prestigious technical journal, calling Friedmann's suggestions "suspicious," and to de Sitter Einstein jotted a note, "This circumstance [of an expanding universe] irritates me." In another note, Einstein reassured one of his colleagues, "I have not yet fallen in the hands of priests," a veiled reference to de Sitter, Friedmann, and Slipher.

In 1925, the American astronomer Edwin Hubble dealt the static model of the universe a fatal blow. Using what was then the largest telescope in the world, Hubble revealed that every galaxy within 6×10^{17} miles of the Earth was receding. Einstein tenaciously refused to acknowledge Hubble's work. The German genius continued teaching the static model for five more years, until, at Hubble's request, he traveled from Berlin to Pasadena to personally examine the evidence. At the trip's conclusion, Einstein reluctantly admitted, "New observations by Hubble . . . make it appear likely that the general structure of the universe is not static." Einstein died in 1955, swayed but still not fully convinced that the universe was expanding.

Ten years later, in 1965, Arno Penzias and Robert Wilson were calibrating a supersensitive microwave detector at Bell Telephone Laboratories in New Jersey. No matter where the two scientists aimed the instrument, it picked up the same unidentified background noise — a steady, three-degree Kelvin (3K) hum. On a hunch, the two Bell Labs employees looked over an essay on general relativity by a student of Alexander Friedmann. The essay predicted that the remnants of the universe's most recent explosion should be detectable in the form of weak microwave radiation, "around 5K or thereabouts." The two scientists realized they had discovered the echo of the biggest explosion in history: "the big bang." For this discovery, Penzias and Wilson received the Nobel prize.

The discovery of the "3K hum" undermined the static model of the universe. There were only two models left: one that worked without God and one that did not. The last issue to be settled was: Had the primordial universe exploded an infinite number of times (the oscillating model) or only once (the open model)? Researchers knew the issue could be settled by determining the average density of the universe. If the universe contained the equivalent of about one hydrogen atom per ten cubic feet of space, then the gravitational attraction among all the universe's particles would be strong enough to stop and reverse the expansion. Eventually there would be a "big crunch," which would lead to another big bang (and then to another big crunch, etc.). If, on the other hand, the universe contained less than this density, then the big bang's explosive force would overcome all the gravitational pulls, and everything would sail out into nothingness forever.

Curiously, the death of the static model inspired panic in many quarters of the scientific world. Mathematicians, physicists, and astronomers joined forces to prove the eternity of the universe. Dr. Robert Jastrow, arguably the greatest astrophysicist of the time and director of the National Aeronautics and Space Administration's Goddard Center for Space Studies, was named head of the research project. For fifteen years Jastrow and his team tried to demonstrate the validity of the oscillating model, but the data told a different story. In 1978 Jastrow released NASA's definitive report, shocking the public with his announcement that the open model was probably correct. On June 25 of that year, Jastrow released his findings to the *New York Times Magazine*:

This is an exceedingly strange development,

unexpected by all but the theologians. They have always accepted the word of the Bible: "In the beginning God created heaven and earth." . . . [But] for the scientist who has lived by his faith in the power of reason, the story ends like a bad dream. He has scaled the mountains of ignorance; he is about to conquer the highest peak; [and] as he pulls himself over the final rock, he is greeted by a band of theologians who have been sitting there for centuries.

Dr. James Trefil, a physicist at the University of Virginia, independently confirmed Jastrow's discovery in 1983. Drs. John Barrow, an astronomer at the University of Sussex, and Frank Tipler, a mathematician and physicist at Tulane University, published similar results in 1986. At the 1990 meeting of the American Astronomical Society, Professor John Mather of Columbia University, an astrophysicist who also serves on the staff of NASA's Goddard Center, presented "the most dramatic support ever" for an open universe. According to the *Boston Globe* reporter covering the conference, Mather's keynote address was greeted with thunderous applause, which led the meeting's chairman, Dr. Geoffrey Burbridge, to comment: "It seems clear that the audience is in favor of the book of Genesis — at least, the first verse or so, which seems to have been confirmed."

In 1998, Drs. Ruth Daly, Erick Guerra, and Lin Wan of Princeton University announced to the American Astronomical Society, "We can state with 97.5 percent confidence that the universe will continue to expand forever." Later that year, Dr. Allan Sandage, a world-renowned astrophysicist on the staff of the Carnegie Institution of Washington, was quoted in *The New Republic* saying, "The big bang is best understood as a miracle triggered by some kind of transcendent power." *Newsweek* columnist George Will began his November 9, 1998, column with this quip: "Soon the American Civil Liberties Union or People for the American Way, or some similar faction of litigious secularism, will file suit against NASA, charging that the Hubble Space Telescope unconstitutionally gives comfort to the religiously inclined." The same year, *Newsweek* reported a recent and unexpected swing of opinion among the once passionately agnostic: "Forty percent of American scientists now believe in a personal God — not merely an ineffable power and presence in the world, but a deity to whom they can pray."

There are, of course, mathematicians, physicists, astronomers, and cosmologists who choose not to believe in God today. For a variety of reasons, they choose instead to have faith that new natural laws will be discovered or that new evidence will appear and overturn the current model of an open, created universe. But for many in the scientific community, the evidence is persuasive. For many, modern cosmology offers permission to believe.

LAWRENCE KELEMEN is the author of *Permission to Believe: Four Rational Approaches to God's Existence* (Targum/Feldheim, 1990) and *Permission to Receive: Four Rational Approaches to the Torah's Divine Origin* (Targum Press, 1996). He studied at U.C.L.A., Yeshiva University of Los Angeles, and Harvard University. He was also a downhill skiing instructor on the staff of the Mammoth Mountain Ski School in California and served as news director and anchorman for KMMT-FM radio station. Currently he teaches medieval and modern Jewish philosophy at Neve Yerushalayim College of Jewish Studies in Jerusalem.

Jewish Mysticism: Unearthing the Spiritual in a Physical World

Ellen Solomon

Life is full of pleasurable experiences: an early morning at the seashore, a favorite piece of music artfully performed, a strong connection with another person. Often, we seek out experiences for the feelings and states they create in us, from the high energy and confidence achieved while climbing a mountain to the inner peace found amidst a gardening project. Whether we pursue solitude or time with others, an international experience or an activity in our own neighborhood, we frequently emerge from these encounters uplifted and rejuvenated.

Jewish literature abounds with positive references to man's experiences in this world. The great medieval commentator Rabbi Moses Maimonides writes about drawing inspiration from daily life: the intensity of "being in love" teaches us about the yearning and love for God; witnessing the beauty of nature develops greater awe of God. The Talmud states that after death we will be asked whether we enjoyed the pleasures of this world during our lifetime and will have to justify ourselves if we did not. In addition, Jewish mystical literature also encourages us to interact with this world, telling us about the holiness, or divine energy, that permeates the physical universe.

The Creation Process

Before Creation, the only thing that existed was God. His essence filled the entire universe, leaving no "space" available for any further creation. Therefore, when it came to the mind of God to create our universe, the Kabbalists (Jewish scholars of mysticism) say He constricted Himself to make room so this world could be created. This act is referred to by the Kabbalists as "*tzimtzum.*"

The *tzimtzum* was not actually the creation of one universe but of many. God formed a progression of concentric universes, each containing a measure of His infinite light, although in diminished concentration, so the universes could exist outside His essence. Each universe received a lesser concentration of divine light than the one created before it. Because of their high spiritual content, each universe was created in the spiritual realm, until the turn came for our universe to be created. This world received an infusion of divine energy with a low enough intensity that it could be represented in a physical form.

Finding the Infinite Light

In our universe, God's essence takes the form of divine sparks. As Rabbi Aryeh Kaplan explains in *Jewish Meditation*, these sparks are the manifestation of God's will that this physical world and everything in it should exist, and therefore these sparks reside in every object and every action. Perhaps the existence of these divine sparks can explain why some schools of meditation use the concentration on a simple phrase or object to achieve a spiritual experience.

Not only can we find mystical experiences within this world, but Jewish mysticism also teaches us that we can sense the light of God beyond this world. In his book *Innerspace*, Rabbi Kaplan says that by meditating on some of the other universes one can experience their spiritual essence. It is possible through prayer or other meditation to perceive the divine energy pouring into this world by way of the worlds beyond.

Man Is Spiritually Active

The Kabbalists teach us that man's role is not one of passive appreciation. Rather, a major element of man's existence is spiritual searching, uncovering the divine energy concealed in the physical world.

The divine sparks in this world lie dormant, and with each constructive action we perform, sparks are released from the physical entities that contained them. Although God's infinite light is mostly hidden in this world, when sparks are released, the divine light permeating our universe takes on a greater intensity. Likewise, destructive actions cause the spiritual light in this world to dim.

The unleashing of sparks in this universe affects the other universes. When divine sparks are set free in this world, it experiences a slight increase in divine light; the quality of light in the world will more closely resemble the original infinite light before the *tzimtzum*. In response to the heightened spiritual level in this universe, the next universe similarly undergoes an increase in spiritual light, causing the next universe to do the same, and so on.

Ultimately, the "message" of our one good deed, transformed by its travels through the spiritual worlds into a highly spiritual communication, reaches God. This is the first half of what Rabbi Kaplan calls a giant "feedback loop," through which God personally responds to our actions. Our universe, as well as the adjacent spiritual universes, does not run on automatic pilot. God, while independent of these universes, remains involved in our lives, responding to our actions with the transmission of infinite light, transformed via the spiritual worlds so that it reaches our universe in the form of additional sparks.

Like all sparks in this universe, these new sparks are concealed in entities around us, waiting for their release to further permeate our environment with spiritual energy. Perhaps this spiritual feedback makes up a part of the pleasure we often feel when performing good deeds and otherwise interacting positively with the world around us.

The Commandments as Tools of Spiritual Communication

Often we have a sense of what is right and wrong, what defines positive or negative action. But sometimes, due to the hidden nature of the divine energy in our universe, we are unaware of many other actions that might be considered good deeds in the spiritual realm.

Fortunately, God did not leave us to figure out the spiritual realm by ourselves. Over three thousand years ago, our ancestors received the divine message called the Torah. The Torah, Hebrew for "teaching," contains stories showing how some Jewish role models lived their lives, as well as the commandments, or mitzvot.

At some point in our lives, many of us have had discussions regarding the relevance of the mitzvot:

"We don't need to keep the commandments; some of them are very outdated. People don't get trichinosis from pork anymore."

"At my house on Passover, each kid got to choose food from their favorite fast-food restaurant. I mean, we still ate matzah to know what it felt like to be a slave."

"Mezuzahs are so nice, reminding us that God is inside the house and all. But why should it have to be a parchment? Any symbol that has meaning should be okay."

Certainly mitzvot encourage people to live healthy and constructive lives. Mitzvot also inspire many of us through their symbolism. But to say that a mitzvah has a single, easily understandable purpose denies its essence.

It is impossible to ascribe only one purpose to a mitzvah. A mitzvah can manifest any number of meanings, depending on the practitioner and his circumstances. Furthermore, each mitzvah has a spiritual impact which we can sense but cannot truly understand. This mystical, unknowable meaning is the true value of a commandment.

Conclusion

Our world is filled with opportunities for spiritual experience. The opportunities are everywhere: close to nature, in a crowd of people, even in the mundane surroundings of our everyday lives. Each of us holds the keys to unlock the divine sparks around us. Through the positive actions of mitzvot, we can fulfill one of human-kind's primary roles: to reveal and enjoy the spiritual elements in the physical world around us.

Ellen Solomon works as a computer programmer in New York City. With a master's in Jewish education, she teaches the laws and ethics of Jewish speech on the Web site www.torah.org.

Freedom Worth Having

Dovid Gottlieb

W̶e all believe that many of the things we do are up to us. Our decisions make the difference. They determine the success or failure of our lives. If we do something without free will — if we are pushed by an external force which compels us — then we feel we are not responsible.

But do we really have free will? There are some concepts within Judaism, and some scientific and philosophical beliefs, which seem to say humans do not possess free will. Let us briefly consider a few of these challenges.

THE CHALLENGE: *"Free will means I make my own decisions. But Judaism teaches that God commands us what we must do. Following God's commands means that I am not making my own decisions; i.e., I really do not have free will."*

THE RESPONSE: There is a difference between the power to act on your own, with no external force forcing you, and the authority to do what you please with no rules or values to limit your choices. Let's call the first "free will power," and the second "free will authority." God's commandments do not take away free will power. Proof: many believers manage to disobey God's commands! Furthermore, we all manage to do what we know is bad for ourselves — bad for our health, our relationships, our studies, and so on. Merely knowing what must be done does not take away free will power. God's commands do take away free will authority, but Judaism welcomes that result. We could put it this way: we have the free will power to be good or evil. We do not have the authority to define good and evil as we please.

THE CHALLENGE: *"Judaism teaches that God created the world. That means He determined what will happen in it. Everything that happens is fated, predestined. That means God's power really makes everything happen. That is the external force pushing us. So we do not even have free will power."*

THE RESPONSE: God created the world, and He created in it the power of free will. He did not predetermine this part — the free will part — of the world (and related parts). He gave us the power to determine it. When you read statements in Jewish sources which sound as if a human action is predetermined, if you check carefully you will see that this is a misunderstanding. For example, we are told that forty days before a child is formed in the womb, a heavenly voice declares that this child will marry So-and-so. Does this mean that our marriage choice is fated? We are also informed that during the days of mourning for the destruction of the Temple, we are forbidden to make any voluntary celebrations except for an engagement. Why is that the exception? Because if you and your future spouse are willing now, clinch it now, since in two weeks something may change and you will miss the opportunity. Obviously the marriage choice is not fated — it could work out in different ways. Judaism rejects the idea that human actions are fated.

THE CHALLENGE: *"God knows the future. That means before I act God knows what I will do. Then I really do not have the possibility of doing anything else. So I really do not have a choice."*

THE RESPONSE: Although this is a difficult question, Jewish sources have no less than four different answers! But none of them is simple. Here I will briefly describe two of them.

1. God is above time. So He can see the whole of time, including what I call the future. He sees what I do. But watching me act does not make me act. His knowledge is the result of my action, which is the result of my choice. It does not limit my choice.

2. Strictly speaking, we cannot describe God at all. He is beyond all conception and understanding. When we seem to be describing God, we are really talking about His actions — how He shows Himself to us, not how He really is. Here is a parallel: Imagine asking someone two hundred years ago what he knows about wood. He answers that wood is flammable, it floats, it comes from trees, takes certain coloring agents, is flexible, and so on. Now you ask why it has these properties — what makes it different from glass, copper, marble, and other materials. What can he say? Two hundred years ago they did not know about molecules. All he can say is that this is how we experience wood, that this is what we observe it to do. But what wood really is, the ultimate structure which explains why it is this way, he does not know. Our relationship to God is something like this.

Now, what do we mean when we say God knows the future? We cannot mean He literally knows it, because we are using the human understanding of knowledge, which, strictly speaking, does not apply to God. We mean only that the world operates under His direction, taking everything in the future into account. But that does not contradict free will power. Only real knowledge would contradict free will power, and we are no longer asserting that.

THE CHALLENGE: *"Social science has shown that we are creatures of our environment. Our culture, socioeconomic class, home environment, schooling, and personal experiences make us what we are. Together these factors are the external force which causes everything we do."*

THE RESPONSE: Social science can only show that these factors influence what we do, not that they cause what we do. The difference is crucial. Though these factors make some decisions harder and some easier, we still have some room to make our own decisions. Statistics prove that children growing up in a decayed urban ghetto are more likely to use drugs, commit crime, and be functionally illiterate than children from other neighborhoods. But these statistics all have exceptions. Some children from the ghettos escape drugs, crime, and illiteracy. Some children from other neighborhoods experience disaster. The statistics show that these environments make good choices harder; they do not show that the environments cause bad choices. So until we are shown a description of an environment which produces the same result every time, something social science has never done, causation has not been proved. And the same holds true even if you add in the contribution of DNA. After all, identical twins raised in the same home do not always make the same life choices.

THE CHALLENGE: *"Science has proved that the brain is just a physical-chemical machine. Everything we do ultimately comes from the brain. So the physical processes which cause the brain to develop, and the stimuli which cause it to react, are the external forces which cause our actions."*

THE RESPONSE: Science has proved nothing of the kind. Roger Penrose of Oxford University (with a Nobel prize in physics) and Sir John Eccles (with a Nobel prize in brain physiology) are among the dissenters. The brain being a machine is an assumption of much contemporary science, but it has never been proved.

I hope this brief discussion has shown you that free will is at least a possibility. But given that we have free will, what are we to do with it?

It is often pointed out that a free public library is of no use to an illiterate, and freedom of movement is of no value to someone so poor that he cannot afford transportation. Similarly, the freedom to go to medical school is of no personal value to someone who has no interest or intention of ever going to medical school. There is a general rule here: The potential value of freedom is determined by what we are able to do with it; the actual value of freedom depends on what we really do with it.

This rule applies to each of us. We each have the freedom to do many things. The value of freedom for each of us will be determined by what you or I decide to do with it. How can we decide which of our options has the greatest value? Try this experiment in your imagination: Suppose you stood at Sinai and personally heard God say, "Keep the Sabbath!" Could you ignore that revelation in making your decisions? Wouldn't that revelation make keeping Shabbat valuable? And the same holds true for the rest of the Torah. Once we are convinced that the Torah is true, it becomes the source of value. Thus our freedom achieves its maximum value if it is used to live a life of Torah. This is what the Torah means when it says: "I am Hashem your God Who took you out of the land of Egypt to be your God." That is why He gave us our freedom — so that He would be our God.

DOVID GOTTLIEB taught philosophy at Johns Hopkins University from 1969–1981. Since then he has been a senior lecturer at Ohr Somayach Yeshivah in Jerusalem. He is the author of *Ontological Economy* (Oxford University Press, 1980) and *The Informed Soul* (ArtScroll/Mesorah Publications, 1990).

The Great Science-Bible Debate

Gerald Schroeder

Creation is in the news almost daily. Not the original Genesis account of creation, but the twentieth century version: the big bang. Skeptics and believers alike want to know if the Biblical description of our cosmic origins can jibe with the scientific account.

There's no way, I'm told, we can squeeze fifteen billion years of cosmology into the six days of Genesis, chapter 1. And then there is the Biblical calendar that reports God creating mankind less than six thousand years ago. Haven't I heard of the Cro-Magnon Homo sapiens fossils from fifty thousand years ago? I'm asked.

On the first question, there is a way; and on the second question, I have heard of him.

Here are the questions I'm asked most frequently and the replies I am able to provide while standing on one foot. (For the two-footed answers I've written a couple of books.)

1. Creation? Yes, creation! Today we call it the "big bang."

In the early 1600s, James Ussher, archbishop of Armagh, Ireland, calculated that the creation of the world took place in the year 4004 B.C.E. On October 23. At high noon. Sounds silly, such precision. But then why should a cleric know about cosmology? And so, not surprisingly, a contemporary of Ussher, the famed astronomer Johannes Kepler, sought to correct him.

Kepler is the scientist who discovered that planets move about the Sun in elliptical orbits and not circles, as had been previously assumed. He knew more than just a bit about the world around us. Kepler calculated that the Creation was not in October of 4004 B.C.E. — but in the spring of that year!

Today their use of the Bible as a tool for cosmological inquiry may seem mightily misplaced. So let me put their "error" into perspective.

In 1959, a survey was taken among leading United States scientists. Among the questions was one querying their estimate of the age of the universe. Of those who replied, the large majority, in fact two-thirds, responded: Age? There is no age. The universe is eternal. Plato and Aristotle taught us that.

Six years later, in 1965, with Penzias and Wilson's discovery of the radiation remnant of the big bang, that fundamental paradigm changed. Science had discovered the echo of our creation. There was a beginning to our wonderful universe.

Questions may arise as to the details of that beginning and whether there are other universes, but the overwhelming evidence is that some fifteen billion years ago, the time, space, matter, and laws of nature that make up our universe came into being from what appears to be absolute nothingness. Human logic and scientific belief had sided with the Greek view of the universe, but it was in error. The three-thousand-year-old claim of Genesis 1:1, that there had been creation from void, had been proven correct. For all the chortling about the exaggerated exactness of Ussher and Kepler, they had been infinitely closer to the truth than the majority of scientists in that 1959 survey.

Make no mistake about it. Science has taken the largest step it has ever taken in closing ranks with the Bible. It has confirmed the first part of the first sentence of the Torah. There was a beginning.

2. Was a day a day back then at the beginning?

It's a good question. Genesis, chapter 1, recounts for us the six days of creation. Day by day, the key events are ticked off. But wait. The Sun does not appear till day number four. So how can there have been days before then? All ancient commentators who deal with the meaning of *day* during the creation week tell us that the term *day* refers to a duration of time, and that duration was twenty-four hours, regardless of whether or not there was a Sun. Those first six days, we are told, were no longer than "the six days of our workweek, but," the commentators continue, "those six days contained all the ages and all the secrets of the universe."

Days containing ages? Sounds strange. Nevertheless, that is what we twice read in Genesis: "These are the generations of the heavens and the earth when they were created in the day that the Eternal God made heaven and earth" (Genesis 2:4); and again, "This is the book of the generations of Adam in the day that God created Adam" (ibid. 5:1).

Generations within a day? It took an Einstein to discover how that could happen. The laws of relativity taught the world that the passage of time and the perception of time's flow varies from place to place in our most amazing universe. A minute on the moon passes more rapidly than a minute on the Earth. A minute on the Sun passes more slowly. The duration between the ticks of a clock, the beats of a heart, the time to ripen oranges, stretches and shrinks.

Wherever you are, time seems normal because your body is in tune with your local environment. Only when looking across boundaries to very different locations can we observe the relativity of time. It is a phenomenon that has been confirmed a myriad of times in laboratories around the world.

We look back in time, studying the history of the universe. From our vantage we find billions of years have passed. And they did. But to understand the opening chapter of Genesis, we must identify its perspective of time. Again the ancient commentators: Why, they asked, is the end of the first day recorded as "and there was evening and there was morning: day one" (ibid. 1:5) and not "a first day"? The remaining days are recorded as "second," "third," etc. "One" is absolute; "first" is comparative.

The Bible states "day one" to teach that this day is near the beginning, the time when the first stable matter formed from the energy of the big bang. It was a moment when no other time existed. By the second day, there was already the previous day with which to compare it, and hence the statement "and there was evening and there was morning a second day" (ibid., 8), second relative to the first day.

Viewing the events of our unfolding universe from that beginning holds the answer as to how our generations fit into those days.

The universe we live in is not static. It is expanding. The space of the universe is actually stretching. If we took a mental trip back in time, sending our information back to the moment from which Genesis views time, the effect of our mental trip would be to pass to a time when the universe was vastly smaller, in fact a million million times smaller than it is today. Space would have shrunk a million millionfold. This huge God of space would equally compress the perception of time for any series of events.

To calculate the effect of that million million compression, we must divide the fifteen billion years we observe looking back in time by the million million. The result: a mere six days passed as viewed from the beginning. Which of course is just what Genesis, chapter 1, has been claiming for the past three thousand years. Genesis and the science of cosmology tell the same account but seen from vastly different perspectives.

3. Evolution in the Bible? You've got to be kidding!

No, the Bible is well aware of evolution, or, to be politically safe, let's call it "development." But the Bible is not very interested in the details of the process. And so it describes all of animal evolution in a mere seven sentences (Genesis 1:20–26). Genesis tells us simple aquatic animals were followed by land animals, mammals, and finally humans. That is also what the fossil record tells us, but of course with much more detail than these few Biblical verses provide.

While the Bible has no problem with the development of life from simple forms to the more complex, neo-Darwinian theory (gradual evolution through random genetic mutations selected for or against by environmental conditions) has many. First came the discovery that life appeared on the Earth almost four billion years ago, immediately after the molten globe had cooled sufficiently for liquid water to form. This contradicted totally the theory of life's gradual evolution over billions of years in some nutrient-rich pool. The rapid origin of life remains a mystery. Then we learned that some 550 million years ago, in what is known as the Cambrian explosion of animal life, every basic body plan that has ever existed burst upon the scene, with no foreboding in the underlying fossil record. It is no wonder that Darwin, in his *Origin of Species*, repeatedly implores the reader (seven times by my count) to ignore the fossil record if we wish to understand his theory.

Taking the data as a whole, the evidence for a purposeful force (i.e., God) helping evolution along is about as strong as the evidence for random mutations coupled with natural selection being the force behind the process. Either way, something exotic is at work.

4. The Bible's calendar puts the creation of Adam at about six thousand years ago. Science says the number should be closer to sixty thousand years. So who's right?

Let's not confuse man with human. The Biblical creation of Adam, humankind (Genesis 1:27), relates to the creation of the human soul (in Hebrew, *neshamah*) and not the human body. The fifteen- hundred-year-old Talmud is replete with descriptions of hominids having the same shape and intelligence as humans.

But they were not human. They lacked a *neshamah*, a soul. Recall that the Talmud was redacted a millennium before paleontology raised the scientific question of pre-human hominids. The Talmud learned of hominids from nuances in the text of Genesis. Science has confirmed the ancient predictions of Genesis.

It may be more than a coincidence that museums make the break between prehistory and history at about six thousand years ago, with the invention of writing. Necessity is the mother of invention. The sudden expansion of clan-sized settlements into cities necessitated commerce and administration, which in turn required record-keeping and hence writing.

Was it the creation of the *neshamah* that enabled clans to reach out and join together into cities? That is a question unanswerable by science.

5. If God wrote the Bible, why doesn't it mention dinosaurs?

In a way the Bible does mention dinosaurs, or, if not dinosaurs, then large reptiles — which is what dinosaurs were. In Genesis 1:21 we learn that God created the big *taninim*. This is the only animal in the entire creation account with a size attributed to it. *Taninim* are occasionally translated as whales, crocodiles, lizards, even dragons. The confusion over the meaning of *taninim* is surprising, since *tanin*, the singular of *taninim*, is a word known in the Torah. In Exodus, chapter 3, God spoke to Moses from the burning bush, telling him to return to Egypt to lead the Jews to freedom. Moses asked God for a sign, and his shepherd's staff turned into a snake, *nachash* in Hebrew (Exodus 4:3). When Moses used the sign in front of Pharaoh, the staff became a *tanin* (ibid. 7:10), which a few verses later was referred to as a *nachash* (ibid., 15). We learn from this that *tanin* is a general category within which *nachash* falls. The general category for snakes is reptile.

Genesis 1:21 reads "and God created the big reptiles." Dinosaurs were certainly big reptiles.

6. Who started this whole controversy between Bible and science?

If I had to choose a single source for this travesty I would be forced to lay the blame on the religious community. Theologians who have the scantest scientific knowledge are willing to trash every scientific discovery related to the cosmos or the development of life that seems to encroach upon some imagined sacred turf.

First Copernicus in the 1500s had the audacity to suggest that the Earth moved around the Sun. This was unacceptable to the religious establishment, notwithstanding that the opening sentence of the Bible places the heavens before the Earth. A hundred years later, Kepler shook the religious world with his discovery that the Earth moves in an ellipse. This humiliated the clergy. Would not a perfect God produce a perfectly circular orbit? The next century brought Newton and the laws of inertial motion. It must have come as a bolt out of the blue for him to find he was accused of bringing "occult qualities" that were "subversive to revealed religion." What subversion? Well, with inertial motion the planets could keep moving by themselves without God's constant push. One would have to search far and wide today to find a cleric who is against the laws of motion. But with each stage, the popular impression was that science had proven the Bible wrong, notwithstanding the fact that the Bible had made no claims in any of these fields.

The topics of the controversy have changed, but the claims remain. Today it is dinosaurs and cavemen. In a world so oriented toward science, it would bode well if the clergy had an inkling of what the claims of science really are. As Maimonides wrote eight hundred years ago in the introduction to *The Guide for the Perplexed*, "The only path to knowing God is through the study of science, and for that reason the Bible starts with a description of the Creation."

GERALD SCHROEDER earned his Ph.D. in earth sciences and nuclear physics from MIT. He is an internationally respected lecturer specializing in subjects relating to science and Torah. He is the author of *Genesis and the Big Bang* (Bantam Doubleday), now in six languages, and *The Science of God* (Free Press of Simon & Schuster).

A Rational Approach
to the Torah's Divine Origin

Lawrence Kelemen

The beginnings of all ancient and modern religions have a common thread: one or two people have a revelation and persuade others to follow. Thus, for example, Buddhist writings tell us that Prince Siddhartha Gautama launched Buddhism after his solitary ascendance through the eight stages of Transic insight; Islamic texts tell us that Muhammad founded Islam following the first of many personal, prophetic experiences; Christian writings reveal that Paul first met Jesus, converted to Christianity, and spread the faith more than three decades after Jesus' death; Joseph Smith, Jr., and his partner, Oliver Cowdery, launched the Church of Jesus Christ of Latter- day Saints (the Mormon church) after the two men were visited by angels and long-dead disciples of Jesus; and Sun Myung Moon launched the Unification Church after privately receiving direct orders to do so from Jesus himself. The beginnings of Children of God, Christian Science, Eckankar, Elan Vital, I AM, and Theosophy — in fact, the beginnings of all world religions — are equally unverifiable. Never does a large, clearly identifiable group of people experience prophecy and live to tell others about it.

Moreover, in a handful of cases wherein large groups of people supposedly witnessed miracles, rarely are these witnesses named or identified in any way that would allow for verification; and in the very exceptional cases involving clearly identified groups of witnesses, never more than one or two of the religion's current adherents claim to have met or descended directly from the named witnesses. In all these cases, the religion's credibility rests on the credibility of its one or two founders. While it is certainly possible that the beginnings claimed by any of the thousands of sects and cults included in the world's more than three hundred major religious traditions could be true, it is easy to imagine how charismatic charlatans could have launched any of these movements.

The one known exception to this rule is Judaism. The Torah claims that every Jewish man, woman, and child alive in 1312 B.C.E. — about three million people, according to the Torah — heard God speak at Mount Sinai and survived to teach their descendants about the event. Here we have an easily identifiable group — all of Jewry — who could have verified or denied the story any time during the first two or three generations after the alleged mass prophecy transpired. While it is easy to imagine how most religious mythologies could have been fabricated and spread, understanding how Judaism could be a lie requires more extensive analysis.

Smart Lies and Foolish Lies

Anyone who has studied history will affirm that people are gullible. We consistently find that sufficiently charismatic leaders can persuade people of any lie, even a lie that obligates followers to engage in painful or self-destructive behavior, *as long as followers cannot check the lie*. Lies that cannot be checked or validated are "smart" lies, insofar as they are maximally seductive. However, claims that can be checked, "foolish" lies, tend to be tested and rejected, especially when the lie obligates followers in unpleasant or suicidal observances.

As an illustration of this principle, consider the case of the California cult known as Heaven's Gate. The group, led by Marshall Applewhite, included seventeen men and twenty-one women between the ages of eighteen and seventy-two. Applewhite taught his followers that he was an alien who first "moved into and took over" Jesus' body just prior to Christianity's founding, and that he again in 1970 "incarnated into" his current human body. In March 1998, Applewhite revealed to his followers a prophecy indicating that an approaching spaceship tailing the Hale Bopp comet was coming to pick up members of Heaven's Gate, but that they would have to take lethal doses of phenobarbital in order to join him aboard the alien craft. On video, members of the group affirmed their faith in Applewhite's vision and then commenced committing suicide. Significantly, Applewhite did not tell his followers that "the spaceship that dropped you (or your grandparents) here on Earth is coming to pick you up." This would be a foolish lie. Applewhite, like all successful religious leaders, told smart lies — lies that couldn't be checked.

Moses Theory and Fred Theory

The claim that three million people heard God speak appears in every intact Torah scroll ever found. The claim is either true or false. If it is a lie, and no such revelation ever took place, at some time in the past someone must have made such a claim. If we contemplate what the scene must have looked like when a false claim of national prophecy was first launched, we find ourselves locked into one of two scenarios: The person making the claim either told his followers (a) that the national prophecy happened in the present — "You *personally* heard God speak" — or (b) that the national prophecy happened in the past — "Your *ancestors* once heard God speak." We might call the first theory "Moses Theory," since the Torah records that "Moses" was the name of Jewry's leader when the prophecy took place. We can call the second possibility "Fred Theory," since the leader during this post-Sinaitic period need not be Moses — he might as well be Fred.

According to Moses Theory, ancient Jewry's leader told a foolish lie: "You personally heard God speak, and He said these words: 'I am the Lord your God. . . .' " We can imagine the scene as people first examined the supposedly divine Torah and their charismatic leader tried to explain to Jewry some of the text's more unpleasant rituals: "Circumcision? Yes, use a very sharp knife and a quick downward motion . . . *and it was the God Whom you heard speak Who told me you should do this!*" People would probably know if they had heard God speak; and if they hadn't heard God speak, they might be a little hesitant to accept the Torah's validity. Because people won't accept foolish (checkable) lies that demand self-destructive behavior, even critics who posit that the Torah is a fictional, man-made document reject Moses Theory.

Those who view the Torah as a work of human imagination therefore put their faith in Fred. They posit that the initial lie was: "God spoke not to you but to your ancestors. He gave them the Torah. They carried the Jewish tradition for a period but then fumbled, and it was forgotten. Now I, Fred, am returning to you your long-lost religious heritage."

When would Fred claim the national prophecy took place? If he said it happened recently — to his followers' parents, grandparents, or great-grandparents — the lie would be checked, discovered, and rejected. Therefore, Fred must claim the national prophecy took place during "ancient times," five hundred or a thousand years earlier.

This is a smart lie insofar as it can't be checked. Followers would understand why they have no memory of a tradition supposedly lost hundreds or thousands of years before. However, followers would reasonably wonder how Fred himself recalls this otherwise forgotten tradition. Fred could explain things, again with a smart (uncheckable) lie, claiming that God spoke to him alone and revealed the Torah's long-lost text and the story of its original revelation at Mount Sinai. Indeed, most modern skeptics gravitate toward a theory like this.

A major problem with this theory is we've never heard of Fred or his heroic resurrection of Judaism. Certainly one of the most significant events in Jewish history would have been the fumble, when world Jewry forgot they were the three million prophets, and the recovery, when Fred reminded the Jews about the national prophecy at Mount Sinai. Yet in an otherwise comprehensive Jewish history we find no mention of such a claim. Jewish texts describe myriad historical crises and the heroes who assisted during these difficult times. We know that Moses brought the Torah down from Mount Sinai, Joshua first brought the Jews into the Land of Israel, David slew Goliath, Solomon built the Temple in Jerusalem, and Ezra brought the Jews back to the Land of Israel after the Babylonian exile. We know that Rabbi

Judah the Prince compiled the Mishnah and that Ravina and Rav Ashi compiled the Talmud. We know about Maimonides, Nachmonides, and hundreds of other stars of medieval Jewry and what their respective contributions were. We possess detailed records about every great Jewish personality, except for one. We don't have any mention of the man who reminded Jewry that they were the only people in human history ever to experience national prophecy, and we don't have any record of the amnesia Fred rescued them from.

Until two hundred years ago (with the founding of the Reform movement), every Jew and member of a Jewish breakaway group (like the Christians, Sadducees, and Karaites) affirmed that ancient Jewry, *their direct ancestors*, had experienced national prophecy at Mount Sinai. Indeed, virtually every Jew alive today can trace himself back to Orthodox relatives (usually within five generations) who believed with all their heart and soul that they were links in an *unbroken* genealogical chain going back to Sinai. Yet not a single ancient or contemporary individual or religious community has any tradition about the man who should have been the second greatest hero of Jewish history: Fred. Why? Calm, unbiased observers will be quick to admit that perhaps there never was a "Fred" who lied about a national revelation; perhaps something supernatural really transpired at Sinai.

(Occasionally people try to pin the title "Fred" on minor players like Hilkeyahu, Shafan, or Yoshiyahu. At best, such attempts are forced and ask the reader to interpret texts with crowbar and mallet in hand. They also require shamefully contrived rationalizations attempting to explain (a) why not one Biblical verse explicitly mentions the key point that the Jews forgot about the Torah and "Fred" reintroduced them to it, and (b) why the name of the second most important Jewish hero (next to Moses) appears in the Bible less often than the names "Pharaoh," "Yeravam," and "Haman.")

Science, History, and the Probability Paradox

The ultimate attack on both Moses and Fred Theories sprouts from the work of physicists and historians. Physicists believe that the laws of nature are constant and can be depended upon, and that therefore natural events will reoccur. Indeed, when faced with a phenomenon that cannot be naturally duplicated, scientists and historians doubt it ever transpired naturally in the first place.

As an illustration, imagine someone exhibited a brick of solid gold and claimed that it was once wood, but that he had used a natural chemical process to convert the wood into gold. Imagine further that twenty thousand chemists were handed a description of the process supposedly used, but that in fifty years of trials not a single experimenter succeeded in duplicating the effect. What would the scholarly community conclude? Precisely because we believe that natural events will happen more than once, we would deduce either that wood never really became gold, or, if the phenomenon really took place, that it transpired supernaturally.

The axiom that natural events reoccur is translated by historians into the principle "History repeats itself." Since history is the story of natural creatures interacting according to natural laws, we expect and do find the same sort of human experiences and responses happening over and over again. Hence religions throughout history and across the globe have produced a strikingly limited set of claims of how they began: *individual* founders of religion have interacted with the gods, sun, moon, stars, oceans, trees, animals; *individuals* claim to have been visited by the dead or by aliens from outer space; and *individuals* claim to be incarnations of divinity. Although the details of theology vary, all of the general claims about how the world's religions began fit neatly into a handful of general categories. There is only one categorically unique claim in mankind's religious history: only the Torah claims that a large, easily identifiable group heard God speak and survived to tell about it.

The Torah is aware of its uniqueness and unabashedly offers this challenge to every Jew who has lived since Sinai:

> You might inquire about times long past, going back to the time God created man on earth [exploring] one end of the heavens to the other. See if anything as great as this has ever happened, or if the like has ever been heard. Has any nation ever heard God speaking out of fire, as you have, and still survived?

> (Deuteronomy 4:32–33)

Crucially, the Torah's claim about national revelation isn't esoteric. If a religion claimed to have started when a centipede metamorphosed into a gorilla who, falling into a river, exploded in flame and disintegrated into ashes before rising in the form of a great human prophet, we would understand why such a claim might never be repeated. It is unlikely that two people would independently dream up identical stories with such intricate and nonintuitive details. Yet the Jewish claim is obvious and simple: God spoke to a group of people.

This is the sort of claim that would occur to anyone.

Moreover, the claim of mass revelation was needed by other religions. Because Jews believed that millions of people — all of their ancestors — received the Torah directly from God, they were hesitant to accept just Jesus or Muhammad's word that the Torah had been annulled. If God changed His mind, Jewry reasoned, why didn't He let us or any other large group of people know? Furthermore, intelligent pagans might have wondered why, if God really intended to reveal an equally acceptable alternative to Judaism, He didn't do it in front of a few million non-Jews. By hesitating to claim a mass prophecy, early Christians and Muslims thus lost an opportunity to raise their credibility, even in the gentile world.

Skeptics who would construct apparently reasonable scenarios explaining Judaism's beginning are thus faced with a paradox: as they become more convinced of any scenario's plausibility, they become increasingly incapable of explaining why no other group seized the obvious, simple, and valuable claim of national prophecy. Maybe one generation of Jews was unusually wily and succeeded in forming and maintaining a national conspiracy. Maybe one generation of Jews were exceedingly gullible and incorporated the whole story without checking their older relatives. Maybe the Jews were developmentally disabled or on a massive drug trip. Maybe thunder sounded like "I am the Lord, thy God. . . ." Whatever scenario we formulate, we face the challenge: if it's natural for an entire people to think they or their ancestors heard God speak, why didn't it happen more than once in history? Just as thousands of failed trials would persuade us that wood cannot naturally be transformed into gold, so too the total absence from history of the most basic religious claim — national revelation — should tell us that people don't naturally come to the conclusion that they or their ancestors experienced prophecy.

We understand the beginnings of Buddhism, Christianity, Islam, and modern cults. We can envision how such faiths started. But how do we explain Judaism's genesis? What rational, natural explanation describes the events leading to the only claim of mass revelation in four thousand years of recorded human history? The proposition that God indeed spoke to the Jewish nation seems at least as probable as the alternatives.

A biography of the author can be found on page 117.

Jewish Prayer: The Adult View

Lisa Aiken

As a child you probably received a sweater or some article of clothing you liked a lot. However, to your dismay, within a year you outgrew it. There was no alternative other than to replace that sweater with a new, larger one.

Our first prayers and notions about God were learned when we were still children. But, unlike our old sweaters, how many of us have thrown out our childish notions of God and prayer and replaced them with more mature ideas?

For example, imagine that you are a three-year-old child, and you want a piece of cake. Your considerations as a three-year-old are "I want cake. I'm entitled to it, and I must have it!" From the viewpoint of a young child, the major function of parents is to gratify the child's wishes. When they don't, the child feels angry and deprived.

Now imagine yourself in the place of the parent. You happen to know that if the child were to eat the cake, he would get sick or lose his appetite for nutritious food for the rest of the day. From the parent's perspective, how would you feel declining the child's request? How great is the difference between the child's feeling and that of the parent!

One of the fundamental differences between how children and adults view the world is that children filter the world primarily through their emotions, whereas adults can rely more on their intellect to make sense of their experiences. Our emotional view of God is often that of the child who wants. We often feel angry at God for hurting, frustrating, or ignoring us. We have to realize that these feelings are reactions to our perception of God, not to the reality of how God acts toward us. We can never get total knowledge of God's motivations. Therefore, when we react to God's denying us what we want, we must rely, at least in part, on our intellectual understanding of His behavior, and also in part on trust in Him.

Adam and Eve: The First Prayers

God created us with the need to pray so we would have a vehicle through which we could forge an ongoing relationship with Him. We see this from the story of Adam and Eve in the Garden of Eden. The Bible tells how the serpent enticed Eve to eat of the prohibited fruit of the tree of knowledge. She then gave Adam the forbidden fruit to eat. God responded by punishing Adam, Eve, and the serpent. Adam and Eve were expelled from the Garden of Eden, and Adam had to work the soil. The serpent was cursed by having to eat the dust of the earth.

But what kind of curse was that? Dust is everywhere, no matter where the serpent might find himself, he would always have plenty of food!

The curse was that the serpent was now self-sufficient. One who is self-sufficient will never approach his Creator to ask for necessities. In other words, God was so disgusted with the serpent He wanted as little as possible to do with him. In contrast, God desired humans to always turn to Him to ask for what they need.

Self-Improvement through Prayer

Prayer is not only a request for physical and material needs, but also a vehicle to transform ourselves into more developed persons. When we lack something, we should do some heavy thinking. What is it that we're missing? Do we really need and want it? If we get what we desire, will we use the gift in a way that God intended: to elevate us spiritually? Without this process, we might simply use our blessings to satisfy our physical or material desires.

Additionally, prayer allows us to forge a relationship with God and make Him a reality in our lives rather than an abstract concept.

These are the benefits that the serpent, as well people who see themselves as self-sufficient, will miss out on since they will not feel compelled to connect with God.

The Need to Verbalize Prayer

One of the tenets of Jewish prayer is that it is not enough simply to "think" a prayer, or to have a certain feeling in one's heart toward God. Jewish prayer requires people to actually say the words. Why? Why can't we just feel something in our hearts and communicate it to God by thinking?

One of the greatest challenges of any relationship is in communicating effectively. Many married couples love each other but cannot communicate that love. Love and communication are not synonymous. If a husband can't express his love to his wife, or vice versa, the love may ultimately erode and eventually be replaced by aloofness or even resentment.

In the same vein, it's not enough to worship God in our hearts. We must also communicate our thoughts and feelings verbally, or they cannot enable us to deepen our relationship with God. When we say what we feel, God becomes more of a reality for us, and we show a deeper level of sincerity about the relationship. No normal person speaks out loud unless someone is listening. Our verbalization concretizes for us that God really hears what we say. In addition, once we verbalize our feelings, they attain a reality that is much stronger for us than had we not committed these feelings to words.

God Meets You Halfway

As much as we yearn to reach a God who at times seems inaccessible, God yearns, as it were, to respond to our strivings. Were our entire task in prayer to try to engage our hearts to talk to God, we might not succeed.

However, the process of prayer is not a one-way street. Once we start talking to God, we demonstrate that we are trying to access Him. Quickly God responds by allowing us to feel His nearness and His reality. The more we allow ourselves to let go of our privacy and share our innermost selves with God, the more we overcome the distance we feel between ourselves and Him.

LISA AIKEN is a practicing psychologist in New York City and Great Neck, Long Island. From 1982–1989, she was chief psychologist at Lennox Hill Hospital in New York City and a clinical assistant professor at New York Medical College. She has lectured for diverse Jewish groups and other organizations in over a hundred cities on four continents, and she has appeared on radio and television. She coauthored *The Art of Jewish Prayer* with Rabbi Yitzchak Kirzner, zt"l, and authored *To Be A Jewish Woman; Why Me, God?: A Jewish Guide for Coping with Suffering; Beyond Bashert: A Guide to Dating and Marriage Enrichment;* and *The Hidden Beauty of the Shema.*

Bringing Up Baby:
A Jewish Education Primer

Dovid Orlofsky

Mazel tov! It's your first baby. . . . So the little baby is home and growing and helping you become better people by overcoming the embarrassment that comes from constantly running to the emergency room every time the baby is constipated. Now begins the next task of a Jewish parent: providing the little one with a Jewish education.

Pre-education

Education begins while a child is lying flat on his back, half asleep. No, I'm not referring to high school. I mean that as the baby is looking around his nursery for stimulation, the environment will teach him things about what is important in life. Is his room decorated with pictures of great sages, of grandparents and great- grandparents, inspiring him with a sense of continuity? Or will he grow up believing that the most important thing in life is a purple dinosaur? Or a six-foot mouse? Or a frog with a banjo who dates a pig? And if so, then doesn't that continue into life, being replaced by the latest media star? Barney turns into Michael Jordan who turns into Robbie Williams who turns into Donald Trump.

The things we use to decorate our children's rooms — and for that matter, our own homes — impress our children with what we value.

A fellow I knew once asked to meet with me to discuss his children. Although he wasn't observant, it was very important to him that his children marry Jewish people. While we were talking he told me about his late grandfather, who had been a Talmudic scholar. His grandfather had left him crates of Jewish books. The man told me that since they were in Hebrew he had no use for them and I was free to take what I wanted. I refused. "Those books are your inheritance," I told him. "If you're worried about who your children are going to marry, then take those books out of the garage and display them in your living room. Let your children see that they're more important to you than valuable antiques or china." The man agreed and displayed the books in his living room for his children to see. (I offered to take the antiques and the china — I already had Jewish books.)

As our children grow we teach them how to say the blessings and prayers a Jew must recite. At this point some parent will complain, "That sounds like coercion!" This is the same parent who spends hours annoying his children with flash cards for math and language skills. Why is it that anything we care about that we force our children to learn is called education, but anything we don't really care about is coercion? If our children said they weren't interested in learning spelling or grammar, would we say we'll let them decide when they're older? No way, because language skills are important. They're part of the "real world." Well, if Judaism isn't important enough for us to instill when our children are young, we've already taught them how important we think it is. Less than "The Itsy, Bitsy Spider," which every parent seems manic about their children learning, with, of course, all the proper movements. Heaven help the small child who can't simulate the part when the rain washes the spider out (which is really a little sick when you think about it — what's next, melt the little ant with a magnifying glass?).

School

Before you know it, the little genius is ready for school. As you might've guessed, the choice of school is going to affect his Jewish education. If you choose a fine secular school and plan to supplement the education with after-school studies, you might as well quit now. What kid is going to enjoy shlepping to extra classes with a bunch of exhausted teachers at the end of a long day while his friends play outside?

This is the time to consider a Jewish day school. This way there's at least a chance that your child will be exposed to the classics of Jewish thought such as the Bible, the Talmud, Maimonides, and the Code of Jewish Law, in the original Hebrew. But won't my child look down at me if he knows more than I do? That depends. If you're secure with who you are as a person and your child's relationship with you, then no, you'll both share the learning experience together. If you're insecure and are dominating and controlling, then yes, you will feel threatened. But you'll probably also feel threatened if your child has any friends or goes away to college or, God forbid, gets married (probably to a girl who will hate you and take your little boy away — you're really starting to sound like a character out of a Tennessee Williams' play).

How should you choose a Jewish day school? Look for a school where the children are happy. Don't worry so much about the facilities, worry more about the staff. Do they love teaching? Do they love their students? Will they fill your child with a feeling of awe and delight for Judaism? That's what you're looking for in a Jewish school. But if there are more rules than smiles, more honor rolls for grades than for good deeds, more tests than questioning, you've found a great private school, but not a great Jewish school.

More than anything, the obligation for educating children is the parents' responsibility. We only hire teachers to help us do our job. We have to take an interest in our children's school work and communicate with the teachers to reinforce the studies at home. Parents who say things like "Who cares what your teacher said? If he knew anything he'd get a real job!" are sending a clear message to their children. I'm not saying teachers are always right, but they're not always wrong either. Make sure you're both working on the same side.

University

Shortly after your child starts high school it's time to start thinking about college. Needless to say we want our child to attend the most prestigious university in the world. Young people must get a good education, we know. Personally, I'm a little more concerned about what's going on during free time, because most of the time they'll be doing nothing even remotely related to school work. I mean, let's face it, the average college student has such a grueling schedule that they sometimes have to attend classes two mornings *and* two afternoons a week! Egad!

So hopefully you've impressed on your child that there should be more to college life than alcoholism, substance abuse, and casual sex. (I'm assuming that as you read this book, you're at least aware that some people consider some of those things not so positive.) University is also the place where your children are going to find someone to spend the rest of their life with, share their most intimate secrets, and make the painful decisions necessary in life. I'm referring, of course, to their accountant. They might also find their first wife or husband there, so you might want to encourage a university with a large Jewish population. That's probably the best way to guarantee that they'll find a proper accountant.

After college comes graduate school, because this kid wants to put off having to work for a living as long as possible.

Lifelong Education

Even after your child is grown, education continues. You give your adult child advice so he can roll his eyes and mumble under his breath and hate you for life when he doesn't listen to you and you end up being right. Don't let that deter you from your responsibility. Telling children "I told you so" is a sacred responsibility, part of our long heritage, along with exiles and pogroms. Jewish parents should also have pithy advice ready to distribute to their children and grandchildren. They will listen politely and then have you tested for Alzheimer's.

DOVID ORLOFSKY was Long Island Director of NCSY (the National Conference of Synagogue Youth) from 1979–88. He presently teaches at Ohr Somayach Yeshivah and lectures all over Jerusalem and the English- speaking world. He is the author of the soon-to-be published *Judaism for the Disinterested Jew or the Last Book You Read before You Assimilate.*

Epilogue

As I look out from the balcony of our home in Jerusalem, I see an amazing sight: mountains, that pictures and descriptions from only a hundred years ago show to have been desolate and abandoned, are now flourishing with greenery and Jewish life. The Jewish people's return to Israel after two thousand years of longing is nothing less than a modern miracle.

Yet even before this physical return to the Jewish homeland fully materialized, we were already known to be a people of miracles, as none other than Mark Twain commented:

> If the statistics are right, the Jews constitute but one percent of the human race. It suggests a nebulous dim puff of star dust lost in the blaze of the Milky Way. Properly the Jew ought hardly to be heard of; but he is heard of, has always been heard of. He is as prominent on the planet as any other people, and his commercial importance is extravagantly out of proportion to the smallness of his bulk. His contributions to the world's list of great names in literature, science, art, music, finance, medicine, and abstruse learning are also way out of proportion to the weakness of his numbers. He has made a marvelous fight in this world, in all the ages, and has done it with his hands tied behind him. He could be vain of himself, and be excused for it. The Egyptian, the Babylonian, and the Persian rose, filled the planet with sound and splendor, then faded to

dream stuff and passed away; the Greek and the Roman followed, and made a vast noise, and they are gone; other peoples have sprung up and held their torch high for a time, but it burned out, and they sit in twilight now, or have vanished. The Jew saw them all, beat them all, and is now what he always was, exhibiting no decadence, no infirmities of age, no weakening of his parts, no slowing of his energies, no dulling of his alert and aggressive mind. All things are mortal but the Jew; all other forces pass, but he remains. What is the secret of his immortality?

(From Concerning the Jews [Harpers, 1899]; see "The Complete essays of Mark Twain" [Doubleday, 1963], p. 249)

Mark Twain's observations are even stronger in our times. Half a century ago, the Jewish people and its traditions were pronounced dead. European Jewish life, so full of study, joy and hope was decimated by the horrors of the Holocaust. "Modern-thinking" people had no interest in perceived ancient rituals. "Free-thinking" people had no time for anything spiritual. Today, however, we are witness to an extraordinary phenomenon. On the one hand, statistics showing the intermarriage and assimilation rates are frightening. On the other hand, people from across the spectrum of Jewish practice, young and old, well-educated and successful in their careers, are exploring their heritage and discovering how much it offers them in meaning, happiness, understanding, and hope.

In order to survive as Jews we need both knowledge and inspiration, and we are finding it. All around us, more and more people are discovering that being Jewish matters.

D.K.